Teacher's Guide to Accompany
MYTHS AND THEIR MEANING

Eric C. Baade

Brooks School
North Andover, Massachusetts

ALLYN AND BACON, INC., Newton, Massachusetts

Rockleigh, NJ   Atlanta   Warrensburg, MO   Dallas
Rancho Cordova, CA   London   Sydney   Toronto

Illustration page 176: Susan Banta

ISBN 0-205-08410-9

Printed in the United States of America

1 2 3 4 5 6 7 8 9 93 92 91 90 89 88 87 86 85

TABLE OF CONTENTS

To the Teacher

This guide is intended primarily to help the busy teacher by providing background material for class discussion and for the assigning of special projects. In a textbook of the size and scope of *Myths and Their Meaning* it has not been possible to include many stories in their entirety, or many alternative versions of myths. The Teachers' Guide attempts to fill in some of this material.

Students will often ask what events led up to a particular incident, or will want to know what happened afterward. Some of the references to myths they may find in literature, art, or advertising may appear to conflict with the stories as they are told in the text. A teacher who has not received extensive training in mythology might have to do extensive research to provide the necessary answers and explanations; often there is simply not time for this. It is hoped that most of the necessary material will be found in this guide.

When possible, outside reading should be assigned in the primary sources: the *Iliad*, the *Odyssey*, the *Aeneid*, the *Argonautica*, the plays of Aeschylus, Sophocles, Euripides, and Seneca, the Eddas, the *Mabinogion*, the *Morte d'Arthur*, and so on. Some students may find these hard going because of their length and the difficulty of their language; if so, it would be a pity to discourage their interest by letting them think of mythology as too difficult or boring. Hence the titles of some more modern works, many written especially for children and young adults, have been included. Consultation with your school librarian will offer many more.

In the answers given at the end of each lesson the sections in brackets are answers which are not found in the text, but which your students may have learned in class discussions which use this guide.

Following the lesson material, on page 173, there is a description of ancient costumes. This can be useful for the preparation of classroom dramatizations.

An Index of Proper Names, with the pronunciations of names not in the Index of the text, has been included at the end of the Guide.

INTRODUCTION
Meaning of Myths

Birth of Myths

The question of the origin of myths remains a vexed one. The Romans, for example, appear to have had no mythology of their own, although they had many legends about their history and ancestry. Before the influence of the Etruscans and Greeks, Roman religion was nuministic, ascribing a certain divinity to animals, inanimate objects, qualities and events. Such "divinities" were those of the sprouted grain, the fruited grain, the diseases of the grain, the hearth, the baby's first cry, etc. Religious duty must have consisted of the attempt to discover what all these *numina* wanted and to provide it for them so as to keep them well-disposed toward the worshipper.

Prehistoric religion can be studied only indirectly, of course, by extrapolating back from the historic period, and by observing the practices and beliefs of present-day primitive peoples — neither method offering much certainty. Hence there are many theories about the origins of religion and myth. Some believe that numinism is the primitive religion of man, which gradually develops into animism (the belief that everything in the universe is endowed with *anima*, "soul"), and that from animism comes the idea of personal gods and their mythology. Others hold that the personal god is the primitive concept, which in some cases degenerates into animism and then numinism.

Not only are the origins of myths shrouded in mystery, but the myths themselves largely defy classification, analysis, and interpretation. The interpretation (so popular in the last century) of all heroes' stories as mythological accounts of the daily or annual adventures of the sun has now gone out of fashion. It is much more usual now to explain them as highly embroidered accounts of historical events, but this approach also breaks down eventually. Most analyses and interpretations discount the artistic creativity of the myth-makers. In the more developed myths of every culture the origin of the story as nature-myth, culture-myth, history-myth, theogonic myth, aetiological myth, etc. has given way to the desire and ability of the human mind to tell a good story. Hence, except ·in the cases of the simplest, least developed myths, it is impossible to sort out the strands of history, folk tale, legend, religious ritual, etc. of which it may originally have been made up.

Why Myths Are Studied

Myths are for the most part "educational" in the deepest sense of the word. Formal education, in which we learn vicariously instead of by direct experience, has, for most of human history, consisted of learning mythology, from the tabus of the savage to Parson Weems' myth of Washington and the cherry tree. It seems odd that the ancient Athenian curriculum consisted only of athletics and music, but less so when we remember that "music" included the study of epic and mythological hymns and odes. "Continuing education" was provided at Athens by the drama, also based entirely on myths.

Education as vicarious experience is natural. We practice it when we slap a baby's hand to keep him from touching a hot light bulb. The mother rabbit practices it when she thumps the baby who fails to follow her tail. In both cases a lesser pain is used to warn the young away from a real danger. Many of the lower animals have a body of knowledge and skills which must be mastered before the young animal is ready to take his place as an adult. Man, of course, has vastly expanded the process. In this country we think it requires twelve to sixteen years. But for most of human history the chief requirement was to learn the myths and legends of the culture. Even today classical, Germanic, Celtic, and Judaeo-Christian mythologies continue to embody much of what the adult western human needs to know. People who know these mythologies usually find that they have a good grasp of psychology, sociology, and philosophy, without necessarily having studied any of these subjects *per se*.

Another reason for studying myths is provided by those myths which are not part of the common store of human wisdom, but which are typical of a particular culture. Perhaps nothing else is so urgent in today's world as our understanding that the alien attitudes of other cultures have as much validity for them as ours have for us, however strange they may seem. Studying their mythologies is an effective and painless way to achieve this. The strangely slighting attitude of the ancient Greeks toward their women, one which we do not share but which is alive in much of the Mediterranean world today, is very clear in their mythology. The Teutonic *Weltanschauung* takes on a new meaning when we see the melancholy of their myths, in which Good is doomed in the end to succumb to Evil. The reinterpretation of myths through the ages can also be instructive.

Hence the two most important lessons which the human child can learn, that all human beings are exactly alike, and that all human beings are vastly different, can both be taught through the study of myths.

Where Myths Are Found

The mythopoeic spirit seems to be more alive in our own age than at any time since the Seventeenth Century. Witness the popularity, even the cult status, of writers like LeGuin, Tolkien, I'Engle, and Richard Adams, and of films like the *Star Wars* series. To some this spirit represents sheer escapism; it may be, however, that we recognize in the myth a kind of truth which transcends mere fact.

Some additional definitions which may prove useful:

Culture-Myth: a story in which Man is taught the arts of life by some supernatural being

Nature-Myth: a story which explains the phenomena of nature

Aetiological Myth: a story which explains the origin of some ritual or custom

Theogony: an account of the origin of a god or gods

Literary Myth: a myth created essentially by one author (though it may draw upon existing mythologies)

Legend: a traditional quasi-historical story, occasionally containing supernatural elements but not involving the personal intervention of a god

Fable: a story intended to teach some principle, in which animals or inanimate objects speak or behave like humans

Allegory: a story which is an extended metaphor, the characters being personifications and the events and relationships representing other events and relationships

Folk Tale: a story handed down by word of mouth among the common people (Webster). Folk tales differ from myths and legends in that their content is not affected by official cults and their themes are culturally very widespread. The most accessible collection of folk tales is that gathered by the brothers Grimm, *Grimm's Fairy Tales*.

It will readily be seen, as the myths in this book are studied, that they contain elements of all of the above classifications. It may be interesting for your students to pick out elements of folk tale, legend, allegory, etc.

PRACTICAL APPLICATIONS

Postcards and prints for the Album of Mythology can often be found in the shops of art museums.

_____ Word Study _____

1. *Janitor* is derived from *Janus,* the god of gates; *June* from *Juno,* queen of the gods; *Thursday* from *Thor,* the Norse god; *ambrosia* was the food of the Olympian gods; *Gemini* ("twins") refers to Castor and Pollux.

2. A *myth* is an account of the deeds of a god or of a supernatural being. It relates a supposed historical event or it serves to explain some practice, belief, institution, or natural phenomenon. *Mythology* means the study of myths. A *mythology* is the system of myths told by a given race. *Polytheism* is the belief in many gods.

_____ Questions for Review _____

1. & 2. They were early answers to man's questions about the forces and processes of nature, the origins of creation, the vicissitudes of human life, the nature of death, etc. Later myths explained the beginnings of human skills and practices and the reasons for religious rituals and tabus. [All of these answers were molded by the human love of a good story, and some later myths were written primarily to entertain or to teach, as works of literature.]

3. Myths were handed down at first by oral tradition and later were embodied in various forms of literature, notably epic, dramatic, and lyric poetry, and still later in· prose tales.

4. All nations and races have their myths.

5. We study myths to enable us to understand the constant references in literature, music, the plastic arts, and everyday conversation; to know the minds of other cultures far removed from us in time or space; and to gain insight into the nature of the human condition. We study them also because they are an important part of our heritage as human beings and represent Man's earliest thoughts on the important questions of human life.

6. It is hard to imagine that there is any poet who has not been influenced by them, though your students may come up with the

names of some who make few direct mythological references (e.g. some of the Seventeenth-Century "metaphysical" poets, some of the early Romantic poets, and a few contemporary poets).

7. They reveal to us the thoughts, attitudes, and concerns of our earliest ancestors.

8. Myths may be found in original works of the peoples who produced them, in the collections of scholars, in later retellings in poetry, drama, or prose, and in the constant references to them in nearly all the arts.

9. They are employed in everyday life by artists of all kinds, in references in conversation, in advertising, and in the many common words which fossilize mythological references.

10. Your students may find a great many. Along with *martial* and *mercurial* go *saturine, jovial,* and *venereal,* all terms referring originally to the influence of one or another planet in the astrological formation of character. All the names of the days of the week, except *Sunday* and *Monday* contain mythological references. Other words and expressions from names and terms in the text can be found in the Index and in the Word Studies throughout the text.

11. Advertisers love to associate their products with qualities of strength, speed, etc. typified by the ancient gods and heroes.

12. Yes. Your students may enjoy reading works by The Inklings: Tolkien, C. S. Lewis, and Charles Williams. Writers who write especially for young people, but whom adults also enjoy, include Alan Garner, Susan Cooper, Lloyd Alexander, and Madeline l'Engle. You might like to assign some of these for outside reading and have the students describe the mythology of them to the class.

PART ONE: MYTHS OF GREECE AND ROME

1   How the World Began

Coming of the Gods

Greek mythology differs from many others in having no universal creator in its creation stories, though various parts of the universe are created by individual divinities. It is also unusual in that its stories never achieved a canonical version, so that poets, playwrights, and philosophers felt free to adapt existing myths and invent variations and even entirely new stories. This means that any text on mythology must choose among a number of different versions, and explains why you or your students may know other versions of the myths than the ones given here. Much as Homer and, to a lesser extent, Hesiod were revered by later ages, their stories of the origins of the gods were not considered authoritative, and other versions appear. For example, some authors tell us that Cronus did not kill Uranus, but only mutilated him. It is also said that the Giants were produced, not from the blood of Uranus, but by Gaea, to avenge upon the Olympians the overthrow of the Titans, and that the Giants attempted to scale Mt. Olympus by piling Mt. Pelion on Mt. Ossa, but were defeated by the thunderbolts of Jupiter. Most authors agree, however, in the belief in three generations of gods: Uranus and Gaea, the Titans, and the Olympians.

    The Titans' importance in mythology does not end with their overthrow. Not only were some spared to play their roles in later stories, but some became the parents of important figures in mythology, even of Olympian gods. Hesiod says that there were twelve Titans, six male and six female (like the Twelve Gods of the Athenians or the *Consentes Di* of the Romans): Cronus and Rhea, Hyperion and Thea, Oceanus and Tethys, Coeus and Phoebe, Crius, Mnemosyne, Iapetus, and Themis. The sun god Sol (Greek Helios) and the moon goddess Luna (Greek Selene) were the children of Hyperion and Thea. Oceanus and Tethys were the parents of the ocean Nymphs, one of whom, Clymene, became, by Iapetus, the mother of Prometheus and Epimetheus (and, in some accounts, Atlas), and another of whom, Perse, became, by Helios, the mother of Pasiphae (wife of Minos and mother of the Minotaur, Ariadne, and Phaedra), Circe, Aeetes, and Perses (father of the goddess Hecate). Mnemosyne was the mother of the Muses. Latona (Leto), the mother of Apollo and Diana (Artemis), was a daughter of Coeus and Phoebe; Mercury (Hermes) was the son of Atlas' daughter Maia.

Some of the names of the Titans do not appear to be Greek in origin. Iapetus is thought to be Semitic, and may be the same as the name of Noah's son Japhet. Cronus may have been a pre-Hellenic god. The story of the swallowing of the children, though not uncommon in other mythologies, seems out of place in Greek mythology. Later ages mistakenly identified Cronus with Chronus, "Father Time," and made the story an allegory: Time devours all things.

It is generally agreed that Jupiter (Zeus) was originally a sky-god, since the name, in both languages, seems to be derived from an Indo-European word for "bright sky." The root appears in a number of words, and occurs in the names of some other divinities, like Diana, Dione, and Juno (Diuno).

Pluto (actually the present active participle of a verb meaning "to grow rich") is a euphemistic nickname for Hades. He is said to be growing rich because everyone eventually comes to his kingdom. He is usually called Pluto because it was felt that there was some danger in naming him. In the same way the most implacable of the divinities, the Furies, were called "the Well-Wishers" (Eumenides). Similarly, some people today will not use the words "die," "death," or "corpse," preferring "pass on," "passing," and "remains."

Four Ages of Man

The Romans believed that the Golden Age coincided with the reign of Saturn, who, exiled by Jupiter to Italy, founded a settlement on the Capitoline Hill in Rome. During the Feast of Saturn, Saturnalia, 17 - 24 December, gifts were exchanged and slaves were allowed to do as they liked, in commemoration of the happy times of Saturn's reign.

It seems clear to the myth-makers of many cultures that man cannot have been created for the kind of universe he lives in. Why does he have the desire and capacity for peace and happiness, when they are so hard to find? In many mythologies there is thought to have been a time and place when man was perfectly happy, such as Paradise in the Judaeo-

Christian beliefs. The Golden and Silver Ages represent this time. The succeeding ages, however, are not merely mythological, because historians also recognize the Bronze and Iron Ages. The ancients knew that they themselves were living in the Iron Age. They believed that the Heroic Age, the period of the adventures of those descendants of the gods they called "heroes," had come between the Age of Bronze and the Age of Iron.

Dowry of Pandora and Punishment of Prometheus

The gifts of Prometheus to mankind, all but fire, are often ascribed to others: horse-taming to Neptune (Poseidon), shipbuilding to Minerva (Athena), and writing to Cadmus.

During the Ages of Gold and Silver, and at the beginning of the Bronze Age, there were no women. Jupiter's creation of Pandora was intended to offset the advantage gained from the gift of fire. Pandora's opening of her box is an obvious parallel to Eve's eating of the fruit, even to the story that she tempts Epimetheus to join her, as Eve does Adam. It is strange that so many mythologies present Woman as a temptress through whom evils come into the universe. Perhaps these stories represent warnings against a reversion to the worship of the Goddess who, in so many parts of the world, seems to have preceded a god as the Supreme Being.

The theory that the change from goddess to god reflects the conquest of an Earth-Mother-worshipping agricultural people by a Sky-Father-worshipping nomadic herdsman people is probably an over-simplification; but the change itself is attested by mythology and folklore. For example, the oracle at Delphi is said to have been won by Apollo from Gaea or Themis. The worship of Rhea/Cybele was feared by men and was forbidden in some places. The original function of the King, as son or consort of the goddess, was to die annually and to be reborn, like the grain (see the stories of Adonis and of Atalanta). In fairy tales, a prince does not stay at home and inherit his father's kingdom, but marries a princess and gains her kingdom. This suggests that at an early period inheritance was through the female line.

The "mother" whose bones are stones is, of course, the Earth-Mother; likewise it is the oracle of Themis, at Delphi, which instructs Deucalion. In some versions of the story, Deucalion and Pyrrha are saved by floating in a chest (the original meaning in English of the word *ark*), like Noah and his family. One of Deucalion's sons, Hellen, became the ancestor of the Greeks (or *Hellenes*, as they call themselves).

PRACTICAL APPLICATIONS

_____ Specific Literary References _____

1. The punishments of Prometheus.

2. The battle for supremacy between the two generations of gods.

3. The first and happiest period of mankind.

4. The reference is to the great size and might of the Titans.

5. Does she not have the fire from heaven; is she without inspiration?

6. Prometheus was the rebel god who defied Zeus in bringing fire to mankind.

7. At the beginning Uranus and Gaea appeared out of primeval chaos.

8. The mixture of all the elements which preceded the appearance of the first gods.

9. The universal deluge which appears in the Old Testament and nearly all mythologies.

10. The Giants in their attempt to storm Olympus were killed by the thunderbolts of Jupiter.

11. The stones cast by Pyrrha after the flood became women.

12. The Titans were the children of Uranus and Gaea.

_____ Word Study _____

1. *chaotic*: from the Greek word for the original undifferentiated mass of elements from which the universe began. *titanic*: from the Titans, some of whom were thought of as gigantic in size. *geology*: The root *ge* is the same as that in *Gaea*. *Cyclopean*: The ancients called any structure of huge stones "cyclopean," imagining that the gigantic Cyclopes must have built it. *cereal*: from the Roman grain-goddess Ceres. *Olympian*: from Mt. Olympus, where the gods of Greece lived.

3. *Dora*: "gifts;" likewise, Theodore, Theodora, Dorothy, and Dorothea all mean "gift of God." *Golden Age*: the first and happiest age of the human race; the term may be applied to any happy or flourishing period. *Prometheus*: foresighted; *Epimetheus*: hindsighted.

4. Zeus/Jupiter, Poseidon/Neptune, Hephaestus/Vulcan, Demeter/Ceres, Hera/Juno, Hestia/Vesta. Hades.

_____ Questions for Review _____

1. A formless and limitless primordial mixture of all the elements.

2. Gaea and Uranus.

3. Titans; Hecatoncheires and Cyclopes.

4. He was killed [or mutilated and overthrown] by Cronus with the help of the other Titans.

5. Cronus/Saturn.

6. He devoured them, all but Zeus/Jupiter.

7. By his children, with the help of the Hecatoncheires and Cyclopes.

8. Zeus/Jupiter.

9. Hades/Dis, Poseidon/Neptune, Hestia/Vesta, Demeter/Ceres, and Hera/Juno.

10. Mt. Olympus.

11. Prometheus and Epimetheus.

12. Gold, Silver, Bronze, [Heroic] and Iron.

13. By bringing them fire and teaching them its uses.

14. By binding him to a crag in the Caucasus and sending an eagle or vulture to devour his liver by day, allowing it to grow back at night.

15. They were enclosed in a box which was entrusted to the first woman, Pandora, with instructions not to open it. She disobeyed and persuaded her husband Epimetheus to join her in opening the box.

16. By a universal flood.

17. No, Deucalion and Pyrrha were saved.

18. By the conversion of stones (the "bones of their mother") into human beings.

2 Gods of the Sky

On Mount Olympus

Some authors picture the gods as inhabiting the sky, rather than the summit of Olympus, but all agree on the magnificence of their dwellings and the essentially untroubled nature of their life. It is the eating of ambrosia (which in Greek means "immortality") which makes them deathless; in their veins, instead of blood, flows a fluid called *ichor*.

Jupiter, Juno, and Vesta

Jupiter's shield (sometimes a breastplate), the *aegis*, was made by Vulcan from a goatskin (that of the goat Amalthea, whose horn became the cornucopia, "horn of plenty"). It was wielded also by Jupiter's daughter Minerva, and occasionally by Apollo. It is represented as fringed with goat hair or with serpents (see illustrations, pp. 44, 128 left, 148, and 160 in the text), or as bearing the serpent-haired head of Medusa. It may simply be the divine version of the primitive thunder machine, a dried hide which was shaken to simulate the sound of thunder when the priests called for rain, inviting the god to imitate the sound with real thunder. The thunderbolt which Jupiter throws is represented in ancient art as a bundle of flames and arrows tied together in the middle.

Although Zeus and Hera occasionally disagreed over the Trojan War in Homer, and he was sometimes constrained to punish her, there is in early writing no hint of the nagging, shrewish goddess who is constantly enraged and vindictive over her husband's many infidelities, which are doubly insulting to her as the goddess of marriage. As the goddess of marriage she has as one of her attributes the pomegranate, symbol of fertility.

The rainbow was thought to be the path which Iris took through the heavens on her errands for her mistress.

Although Vesta/Hestia is such an important goddess, she seems never to have progressed much beyond a simple personification of the hearth. We know only that she was born of Saturn and Rhea and that she was wooed by, and refused, Neptune and Apollo. It is thought that these virgin goddesses were those whose cults never gave way to the worship of male divinities; and it is true in her case that her rituals were carried out entirely by women. The Vestal Virgins at Rome probably represented, for the city as a whole, the unmarried daughters whose duty it was, in every household, to make sure that the fire never went out. In early times the rekindling of a fire was a difficult business, both physically and ritually.

Children of Jupiter and Juno

The text describes the Greek Ares rather than the Roman Mars; the two were not fully identified until later. Mars was (with Jupiter) one of the two chief gods in Italy. He was originally a god of agriculture and more kindly (hence more popular) than the quarrelsome Ares. He became a god of war because the object of early Italian warfare was the burning of the enemy's crops and the protection of one's own. In early Greek warfare the object was to confront the enemy and make him run away; hence Ares was a much more frightening god. Mars' animals are the wolf and the woodpecker, rather than the dog and vulture. As the father of Romulus, he was especially the protector of the Romans. As a Roman god, he has practically no mythology until his later identification with Ares.

In some accounts Hephaestus (Vulcan) was the child of Hera (Juno) alone, borne by her in emulation of Zeus' production of Athena. He was so misshapen at birth that she cast him from heaven, and he spent nine years with the sea-nymphs in a cavern below the sea. He was recalled to Olympus after he had sent his mother a magical throne which imprisoned anyone who sat in it. He eventually released her and they were reconciled. He was always her partisan in her disagreements with Zeus.

Vulcan may have been thought of as lame because in early village society the smith was perhaps usually a lame man, someone with well-developed arms but unable to farm or fight. His consort is variously said to be one of the graces (Charis or Aglaia) or Venus/Aphrodite. Since he is always described as ugly, this seems odd. But it may merely be an allegory of the ugliness of ore being turned into beautiful metal objects.

Hebe was known to the Romans as *Juventas*, and was for them the patroness of the young men of the Knightly Class who belonged to a kind of club called *Juventus*.

Ganymede was the son of Tros from whom Troy was named. Jupiter gave his father some marvelous horses in exchange for him. He is identified with the constellation Aquarius.

Other Children of Jupiter

Apollo is the only important Greek god who had no Roman counterpart. His worship came early to Italy where he became very popular. The Romans began consulting his oracle at Delphi early in their history. The role of Diana/Artemis as goddess of hunting springs from her earlier function as goddess of untamed nature, which made her also (though a virgin goddess) a fertility goddess. The fertility goddess of Asia Minor was identified with her ("Diana of the Ephesians").

Aphrodite seems to have been originally a near-Eastern fertility goddess. She may have come to the Greeks from the Phoenicians, via Cyprus, another island where she is said to have stepped ashore after her birth from the foam, and from which she is sometimes called Cypris. She is naturally identified with Venus, the Roman goddess of spring and gardens. Venus was important to the Romans as the mother of Aeneas (another indication of her Asiatic origins) and the ancestress of Julius Caesar.

Athena is also a goddess of war, no doubt as the counselor of rulers, but of wise leadership, not, like Ares, of courage or war-frenzy. The Romans easily identified her with their Minerva, goddess of wisdom, arts, and crafts, but did not really think of her as a war-goddess. (They had their own Bellona.) Athena/Minerva is represented as the favorite child of her father, the only deity allowed to borrow his thunderbolts. One very strange account makes her the child of Zeus and Metis ("Counsel"), a daughter of Oceanus and Tethys, Zeus' first wife, whom he swallowed in fear that she would bear a son greater than he, which explains her birth from his head. Athena's apparently non-Greek name suggests that she was one aspect of the pre-Greek Goddess, who appeared as the Maiden, the Mother, or the Crone. Her virginity shows that her worship was never invaded by the cult of a male god, just as her shrine in Athens never fell (as archaeology tells us) to the invaders.

On the first day of his life, Hermes invented the lyre by stretching strings across the shell of a tortoise which he found near the cave in which he was born. He then stole some cattle belonging to his half-brother Apollo. Knowing the thief by his prophetic skill, Apollo accused the baby in his cradle to Zeus, who ordered Hermes to restore the cattle. Apollo, however, was so pleased with the lyre Hermes gave him that he let him keep the cattle and became his friend. Hermes/Mercury was the god of trade and profit, as well as of thievery and lying, and is often depicted holding a purse. Hermes may be another god who had no Roman counterpart. The Romans simply gave him another name, derived from the root which gives us such words as *mercantile* and *commerce*.

Minor Deities of Olympus

Literary references to the Muses often mention their favorite haunts: Mt. Olympus and the Pierian spring; Mt. Helicon in Boeotia, with its two springs, Aganippe and Hippocrene; and Mt. Parnassus near Delphi, with the spring of Castalia at its foot. They may have originated as the nymphs of springs whose waters inspired prophetic utterance, like their Roman counterparts, the *Camenae*, who were in addition goddesses of childbirth. The most interesting myth of the Muses is one which tells how the Sirens, originally winged, lost their wings and leapt into the sea as a result of having tried to compete with the Muses in song. It is odd to find a patroness of astronomy among her musical and literary sisters, but Urania may have been assigned this function because of her name, which means "heavenly." Milton, in *Paradise Lost*, makes her the Muse of theological poetry. All the Muses' names are appropriate to their functions: Clio, "making famous;" Euterpe, "gladdening;" Thalia, "flourishing" (she was the Muse of bucolic poetry, as well as of comedy); Melpomene, "singing;" Terpsichore, "delighting in dance;" Erato, "lovely;" Polyhymnia (or Polymnia), "many-hymned;" and Calliope, "beautiful-voiced." A *Museum* was originally a temple of the Muses.

The Fates were said to be the daughters of Jupiter/Zeus and Themis. Their names mean respectively "the Spinner," "the Allotter," and "the Unavoidable." They are also goddesses of childbirth, and Catullus depicts them as singing, at the wedding-feast of Peleus and Thetis, a song foretelling the birth and future greatness of Achilles. The most interesting myth concerning the Fates is the story in which Apollo, disguised as Hermes and carrying wine which he pretends is the magic potion which keeps Aphrodite young and beautiful, gets them drunk and persuades them to extend the life span of Admetus.

Dike, also called Astraea, lived on earth until the end of the Age of Silver, when she departed for Heaven. She is identified with the constellation Virgo. The Graces are daughters of Zeus. They are assigned many names but are usually called Euphrosyne ("Joy"), Thalia ("Bloom"), and Aglaia ("Brightness"). They are goddesses of grace, charm, and beauty, and are friends of the Muses. The Seasons are called, in both Greek and Latin, *Horae*, which may also be translated as "Hours." All these goddesses, along with Nemesis and Victoria, are essentially personifications, and hence have little or no mythology.

Excavation has shown that there cannot ever have been at Delphi a fissure releasing volcanic vapors. The story was widely circulated in antiquity, however, presumably in an attempt to explain why oracular powers came to the priestess at just that place. Modern visitors have felt that the breathtaking beauty of the site is enough to explain the odd feeling that a divinity is nearby.

When a priestess, called Pythia (from Python), died, a new Pythia became inspired by the god somewhere in the neighborhood and was sought and found by the priests. In the modern view this must have been some unfortunate girl with a mental or physical affliction which caused her to speak incomprehensibly. Her babbled answers to the questions were interpreted and written down by the priest, in verse for ambassadors and important persons, in prose for the rest.

Delphi far outranked the other oracular sites in its prestige, largely, we must assume, because of the intelligence of its priests. They must have had a worldwide intelligence service. They normally directed new colonies to their destination and they always seemed to pick spots which were just right for each city. Their cleverness appears best, though, in the ambiguity of their responses. Whenever they did not feel sure of the correct answer they gave one which would be correct whatever happened. Many of the Delphic responses have been collected and, except for questions of mere fact, they display this clever ambiguity. For example, when King Croesus of Lydia asked if he should attack the Persians he was told that if he did he would destroy a mighty empire. When on his defeat he complained that he had been misled, he was told by the god that it was his own empire that had been meant.

Delphi is a site well worth visiting, not only for the beauty of the place but for the interesting and beautiful remains of architecture and sculpture.

PRACTICAL APPLICATIONS

_____ Specific Literary References _____

References to the Major Gods

1. Ambrosia and nectar are the food and drink of the gods [it is eating ambrosia that makes them immortal].

2. Diana is usually depicted as armed with the bow and quiver and in motion as if in pursuit of her quarry.

3. Jove is another name for Jupiter. Since he was thought to enforce vows made to him more strictly than some of the other gods, the most solemn vows were taken in his name.

4. Juno's bird is the peacock.

5. Mars appears here as the god of war.

6. "Foot-feathered" (referring to his winged sandals) is a common epithet for Mercury in both Greek and Latin.

7. This is a reference to the alternative version of the birth of Venus in which she is born of the seafoam and brought to the shore of Cythera or Cyprus on a seashell.

8. The reference is to Jupiter [in his aspect of Jupiter Pluvius] as the bringer of rain.

9. The passage refers to Diana in her aspects as goddess of the chase, as mistress of beasts, and as a virgin goddess.

10. & 11. Juno is the goddess of married love.

12. Olympian: god-like, awe-inspiring, reverend.

References to Lesser Deities

1. Ganymede, because of his beauty, was chosen by Zeus as his cupbearer.

2. The nymphs inhabit bodies of water, mountains, caves, and trees. [The Graces endow gods and mortals with grace, charm, and beauty. The Nymphs, the Graces, and the Hours or Seasons are often depicted in literature and art as dancing, sometimes together.]

3. Hebe ("Youth") was the cupbearer of the gods before Ganymede.

4. Keats thinks of the rainbow as Iris' bow [but in antiquity she was usually not thought of as armed; the rainbow was her path through the sky.]

5. The reference is to the Muse as the inspirer of poetry.

6. ["The Seasons" and "the Hours" are both translations of the same word (Horae in both Greek and Latin). The dance of the Horae is a metaphor for the constantly recurring pattern of hours or seasons.]

7. The reference is to the separate functions (implied in their names) of the three Fates.

8. See #2. [The Hours, daughters (according to Hesiod) of Zeus and his

second wife Themis ("Law-and-Order") were Eunomia ("Good-Laws-Well-Obeyed"), Dike ("Justice"), and Irene ("Peace"). They were attendants of Aphrodite and hence were often joined with the Graces.]

9. Ganymede is often called a "page" from the Middle Ages on, since the feudal page's duties included acting as cupbearer for his master.

10. See #5.

11. It is a convention from Homer on for epic poets to appeal to a Muse or the Muses. Spenser appeals to the Muse of history because he is about to trace a genealogy.

12. Here "Olympian" has another of its meanings, implying lofty detachment from human affairs.

_____ Word Study _____

1. *Mars* was the god of war. *Iris* was the goddess of the rainbow. *Vulcan* was the god of fire in all its useful manifestations. [A *Museum* was orginally a temple of the Muses; the name was next applied to the university which the Ptolemies built in Alexandria; then it came to mean what it does today. In the same way, an intellectual center is often called an *Athenaeum*, "Temple of Athena," and a theatre the *Palladium*, "Temple of Pallas" or the *Orpheum* "Temple of Orpheus."] From *Nemesis*, the goddess of just anger and punishment. *nectar*: from the drink of the Olympian gods. [The Muses, thought of as dwelling on various mountaintops, were called *Parnassians* from Mt. Parnassus, their favorite haunt.]

3. January (Janus), March (Mars), June (Juno).

4. *jovial*: [In astrology a person born under the influence of the planet Jupiter (= Jove) was thought to have a jovial personality; others might be saturnine, mercurial, etc.] *vestal*: from Vesta, the goddess of the hearth, who was served by a kind of pagan nuns. *volcano*: from Vulcan [in Italian *Volcano*], whose workshops were in volcanoes. *mercury*: Because of its peculiar properties (it is the only metal which is liquid at normal temperatures, it readily clings to other metals, etc.), mercury was important to the ancient alchemists who named it for their patron god. In giving the metal its name they may also have been influenced by the quickness with which it darts about, like the god Mercury. *calliope*: The steam-calliope was rather grandiosely named for the Muse of epic poetry. [Since epic was sung or chanted, it was a branch of the art of music.]

5. Cupid.

_____ Questions for Review _____

1. On the borders of Macedonia and Thessaly.

2. Jupiter, Juno, and Vesta.

3. Jupiter: King and Father of gods and men, god of the sky and the weather, of kingly power, government, law, order, and justice. Juno: sister and wife of Jupiter, goddess of marriage and married love. Vesta: goddess of the hearth and all that it symbolizes.

4. Jupiter: thunderbolt, aegis, eagle, oak. Juno: peacock, cuckoo, pomegranate. Vesta: the hearth and the home-fire.

5. Ares/Mars, Hephaestus/Vulcan [though in some accounts he is a son of Juno alone], and Hebe/Juventas.

6. Ares: war and the battle-frenzy; spear, shield, torch, dog, vulture. [Mars: the growing grain, war; spear, shield, wolf, woodpecker.] Hephaestus/Vulcan: fire, especially the smithy fire, volcanoes, masculine crafts; hammer, tongs. Hebe/Juventas: youth, young men, cupbearer of the gods; wine-cup, wine-pitcher.

7. Apollo, the Muses, Artemis/Diana, Aphrodite/Venus (sometimes said to have been born of Uranus and the sea-foam), Athena/Minerva, Hermes/Mercury.

8. Apollo: the sun, song, music, prophecy, disease, and healing [also archery, flocks and herds, and civic government]; bow and quiver, lyre or cithara [laurel, palm-tree, wolf, mouse, dolphin, swan, hawk, raven or crow, snake]. Muses: Clio: history [scroll or chest of books]. Euterpe: lyric poetry [double flute]. Thalia: comedy [and bucolic poetry; comic mask, ivy wreath, shepherd's staff]. Melpomene: tragedy [tragic mask and high boots, ivy wreath, club of Hercules, sword]. Terpsichore: dance [lyre and plectrum]. Erato: erotic poetry [small lyre]. Polyhymnia or Polymnia: sacred song [veil]. Urania: astronomy [celestial globe and pointer]. Calliope: epic poetry [wax tablet and stylus]. Artemis/Diana: the moon, diseases, healing, the chase [wild nature, childbirth, young children, maidens, nymphs]; bow and quiver, veil and crescent, stag [spear, hunting dog]. Aphrodite/Venus: love and beauty; dove, sparrow [swan, swallow, mussel, dolphin, tortoise, ram, he-goat, hare, myrtle, rose, poppy, apple]. Athena/Minerva: wisdom, war, government, arts and crafts, weaving [spinning, thunder and lightning, horse-taming, ship-building, music (especially the war-dance), agriculture]; aegis, owl, olive-

tree, shield [lance, helmet, gorgoneion, golden staff, spindle and distaff]. Hermes/Mercury: thieves, rascals, heralds, travelers, oratory, gymnastic games, the newly-dead [commerce and profit, sacrificial animals, dice-games, mining, buried treasure]; winged cap, winged sandals, caduceus [palm-tree, tortoise, the number four, fish].

9. Nine.

10. Clio, Euterpe, Thalia, Melpomene, Terpsichore, Erato, Polyhymnia or Polymnia, Urania, Calliope.

11. Omnipotent.

12. Apollo, Artemis/Diana, Aphrodite/Venus, Athena/Minerva, Hermes/Mercury.

13. Certain geographical locations or physical objects which marked an opening in the barrier between divine power and the human world. Each oracle was under the control of the priesthood of a particular god or demi-god. The oracles gave the responses of the gods to mankind by various means.

14. At Delphi and at Dodona.

3 Stories of Jupiter and Minerva

Europa and Her Kin

The origins of the Cretans are as mysterious to history as they are to mythology. Even their language has not been deciphered or even identified. In the myth, Europa found a king, Asterion, already reigning in Crete, and eventually married him. Even the most sceptical of the ancient writers did not doubt that one of her children, King Minos, was a historical figure, who early established his control of the sea and built the great palace the considerable remains of which can still be seen at Knossos. He protected the island with his navy, and Minoan cities, unlike their Mycenean contemporaries, were unfortified. This absence of apparent protection may have led to the story of Talos, a gigantic robot of bronze, given by Hephaestus to Minos, which walked around the island three times a day and threw stones at trespassers. If this failed to frighten them away, he heated himself red-hot and clasped them to his bosom. On the Argonauts' visit to Crete Medea magically removed a plug from Talos' heel, releasing the magical fluid which enabled him to move about.

The righteousness of Minos, which earned him his appointment as one of the judges of the dead, is not obvious in his mythology. In his contest with his brother Rhadamanthus for the kingship, he prayed to Poseidon for a bull to sacrifice. When a beautiful white bull rose from the sea, he cheated the god by sacrificing another, less valuable bull. Poseidon retaliated by causing his wife Pasiphae to fall in love with the bull, by which she became the mother of the Minotaur. His behavior in his war with Megara and Athens seems equally unjust. His son Androgeos, attending the first celebration at Athens of the Panathenaic Games, defeated all the Greek champions. King Aegeus in his anger sent him to attempt to kill the Marathonian Bull. This monster was the same bull which Minos had failed to sacrifice, brought to the mainland by Hercules in his Seventh Labor and later captured and sacrificed by Theseus. When Androgeos was killed, Minos defeated Athens in war and demanded the annual tribute of seven youths and seven maidens. On his way he took Megara (which could never fall so long as its king, Nisus, had a lock of red hair) by persuading Nisus' daughter, who was in love with him, to cut off the lock. In exchange he promised to take her with him. He kept his promise by chaining her to his ship and dragging her through the water until, on the point of drowning, she was changed into a sea bird.

Of Rhadamanthus mythology has little to say: driven by Minos from Crete, he fled to Thebes where he married Alcmene after the death of Amphitryon and became a tutor to the young Hercules. The third brother, Sarpedon, fled to Lycia where he became king. He must have lived to a ripe old age since he fought in the Trojan War, variously reckoned to have occurred three to six generations after his flight from Crete.

The word *labyrinth* is a pre-Greek word which seems to mean "the house of the *labys*." The *labys*, or double axe, is a symbol found in the decoration of the palace at Knossos. It may well be that early Greek visitors found the complexity of the palace's plan (which far surpassed that of Mycenean palaces) so bewildering that it became for them the trackless maze of the myth.

The maze or labyrinth appears to be a powerful symbol not only in classical cultures, but all over the world. It is often by tracing the windings of a maze that one enters (or contacts the denizens of) the Lower World. In this connection it is interesting that Virgil describes the doors of the temple of Apollo at Cumae, which Aeneas visits just before his visit to the Lower World, as decorated by Daedalus with a representation of the Cretan labyrinth.

Virgil also compares to the Cretan labyrinth the intricate winding course followed by the Trojan youths in their ceremonial close-order drill on horseback, a ceremony which he offers as the origin of the Game of Troy performed by upper-class boys in Rome and other Roman cities from the time of Augustus. This labyrinthine pattern may have had something to do with appeasing the infernal gods, since at Pompeii it was called the "Game of the Snake," perhaps in reference to the serpentine pattern of the horse-drill, and because serpents are often associated with the Gods Below.

It is astonishing that the turf-mazes (used for playing a fox-and-geese type of game) which were at one time common in English villages generally had the name "Troy-town," since the naming goes back much too early to be a based on the reading of Virgil. It may be that they embodied a reminiscence of the Roman occupation of Britain where well-born boys must have played the "Game of Troy."

The labyrinth appears in both the wall paintings and graffiti of Pompeii; and, somewhat more surprisingly, formed part of the decoration of many medieval cathedrals, usually as part of the pavement.

A student who wishes to make a report on mazes and labyrinths might like to read *Mazes and Labyrinths, Their History and Development*, by W. H. Matthews.

Daedalus, a great-grandson of the first king of Athens, was not only an architect (builder of the Labyrinth and the Dancing-Floor at Knossos, the Temple of Apollo and the retreat of the Sibyl at Cumae in Italy, and of various reservoirs, heated baths, and fortresses in Sicily) but also the inventor of carpentry, having been the first to devise the axe, the awl, the spoke-shave, the plumb-line, the level, the auger, and glue. To him also were attributed many ancient wooden statues, including one of Hercules, carved in gratitude for the latter's having buried the body of Icarus. Daedalus' apprentice, his nephew Perdix, soon surpassed his teacher, inventing the saw (inspired by observation of the jawbone of a snake), the lathe, and the potter's wheel. In jealousy Daedalus threw Perdix from the top of the Acropolis, but Athena, patroness of craftsmen, changed him into the bird which bears his name, the partridge. Found guilty of murder, Daedalus fled to Crete. Having incurred Minos's enmity by assisting Pasiphae in her liaison with the bull, he flew to Cumae whence he migrated to Sicily. He was received by King Cocalus, whose daughter fell in love with him. She lured Minos, who had pursued him, into a heated bath built by Daedalus, and steamed or boiled him to death. Minos had discovered Daedalus' whereabouts by offering a reward to anyone who could thread a thread through all the windings of a spiral shell. Hearing of the reward, Cocalus presented the problem to Daedalus, who solved it easily by boring a hole in the small end, tying one end of a thread to an ant and putting the ant in at the open end, blocking its return that way.

If it was not Cadmus who brought the alphabet to Greece, the letters at least certainly came from the Phoenicians. The forms, and in some cases the sounds, of the letters are different from those of the Semitic alphabet, but the names of the Greek letters are mostly Semitic. Students who know the Hebrew alphabet might like to report on the derivation of alpha, beta, gamma, etc. from aleph, beth, gimel, etc.

In most accounts the serpent slain by Cadmus was in fact a son of Mars, so that the warriors who sprang from its teeth were his descendants. They showed their martial nature by fighting among themselves until all but five were killed. These became the ancestors of the nobility of Thebes, who called themselves the Spartoi, or "sown men."

Cadmus' wife Harmonia was the daughter of Mars and Venus. All the Olympians attended their wedding.

Oedipus

Oedipus' misfortunes may have been the greatest of those of Cadmus' descendants, but tragedy came to all of them. His son and successor, Polydorus, died young. His daughter Semele, loved by Zeus, was taunted by her jealous sisters about her mysterious lover (a theme properly of the folk tale rather than the myth: for example *Beauty and the Beast* or *Cupid and Psyche*). She made Zeus swear by Styx to give her whatever proof she might demand, and then asked to see him in all his glory. When he reluctantly complied, she was consumed to ashes. When King Pentheus, son of Semele's sister Agave, refused to admit to Thebes the worship of Semele's son, Dionysus, the god maddened Agave and her two remaining sisters so that, in their frenzied bacchic wanderings on Mt. Cithaeron, they mistook Pentheus for a mountain lion and tore him to pieces. His mother carried his head back to Thebes in triumph. Her sister Ino was cruel to her stepchildren, the son and daughter (Phrixus and Helle) of her husband King Athamas. When they fled on a flying golden ram, he became mad, killed her son Learchus and drove her to leap into the sea with her son Melicertes. They both became sea-divinities, she Leucothea and he Palaemon (though, oddly enough, his name appears to be the same as that of the Phoenician Hercules, Melkart). Actaeon, the son of Autonoe, the fourth sister, while hunting, caught sight of Artemis bathing. Because of this, he was changed to a stag and torn to pieces by his own hounds.

Dio Chrysostome, a philosopher of the time of Trajan, believed that Oedipus' tragic flaw was not an over-active intelligence, but rather stupidity, writing that Oedipus' answer to the riddle of the Sphinx was in fact the wrong one, and that she killed herself in disgust expecting not the simple answer "Man" but a philosophical disquisition on the nature of Man.

Callisto and her Son

Lycaon, Callisto's father, was on friendly terms with Zeus and occasionally entertained him at meals. Wishing to find out if the god was really omniscient, he on one occasion killed his grandson Arcas and served his flesh to Zeus at table. In his wrath Zeus destroyed the house with a thunderbolt, turned Lycaon into a wolf, and restored Arcas to life, to become the ancestor of the Arcadians. It was after this that he came so close to killing his mother.

In another version of the myth, Callisto is a nymph of Artemis, who transforms and kills her in a rage at her unchastity.

Baucis and Philemon

Stories of other-worldly beings traveling the earth in disguise are very common in mythology, folklore, and science fiction. There were other tales of Jupiter and Mercury in disguise, and these must have appealed to some deep-seated longing of the human heart. When St. Paul and St. Barnabas cured a cripple at Lystra, a small town of Lycaonia, the villagers hailed them, much to their embarrassment, as Zeus and Hermes.

Another folklore theme which appears in the story of Philemon and Baucis is that of the never-failing pitcher: when the old people pour wine for the gods, they are amazed to find that the pitcher never becomes empty.

Two Contests of Minerva

Visitors to the Acropolis in Athens are still shown the marks of Poseidon's trident in the rock. This myth may represent an unsuccessful attempt of invaders to replace the worship of the Goddess with that of a male god.

The story of Arachne is not told by Greek, but only by Roman writers. It may, like many of the more sophisticated nature-myths, be a late invention. Arachne's name is derived from the Greek word for "spider," *arachnes*, not the other way around. In zoology spiders belong to the class Arachnida.

PRACTICAL APPLICATIONS

Specific Literary References

1. Cadmus and his wife Harmonia were metamorphosed into serpents because Cadmus had slain the serpent [which was Ares' son].

2. Fear can blight our ambitions just as the sun melted the wax which held the feathers of Icarus' wings together.

3. The flight of Icarus is a metaphor for ambition which aims too high.

4. Juno pursued with great vindictiveness not only her rivals but their children as well. [Dryden, however, refers especially to her persecution of Aeneas, whom she hated for other reasons].

5. A reference to the armed warriors who sprang up from the earth when Cadmus sowed the teeth of the serpent [a son of Ares] which he had killed.

6. [As Zeus Xenius] the god is the protector of strangers and [as Zeus Hikesius] of suppliants.

7. Rhadamanthus, along with Minos [and Aeacus], is a judge of the dead, deciding on their punishments and rewards in the Lower World.

8. Zeus Xenius (Jupiter Hospitalis) is also the patron of the guest-host relationship.

9. Athena is the inventress of the olive tree which is sacred to her.

10. Oedipus' name is sometimes used by antonomasia to mean "solver of riddles" because of his having solved the riddle of the Sphinx.

_____ Word Study _____

1. *Europe*: named, according to the myth, for Europa, sister of Cadmus. *Icarian Sea*: supposedly named for Icarus, who fell into it when his wings failed. *Europa*: the moons of the planet Jupiter are named for some of those whom the god loved: Adrastea, Amalthea, Io, Ganymede, Callisto, Leda, etc. A student interested in astronomy might like to make a report on the naming of the planets and their satellites. *Great and Little Bear*: constellations identified with Callisto and Arcas. *Athens*: the city and its patron goddess have the same name.

3. *labyrinth*: a name for the great palace of Minos [at Knossos, meaning "House of the Double Axe." The complexity of its plan made the more primitive Greeks think of it as a kind of maze.] *spider*: *arachnes*, from the story of Arachne and Athena. [*Athenaeum* is the Greek and Latin word for a temple of Athena, goddess of wisdom. A bust or statue of Athena was a favorite ornament for a library in antiquity].

4. What creature is it that in the morning goes on four feet, at noon on two, and at night on three? [Another famous ancient riddle, which was supposed to have caused the death of Homer from chagrin at his inability to solve it, is, "What we caught we threw away; what we could not catch we kept."]

_____ Questions for Review _____

1. Phoenicia, on the levantine coast of the Mediterranean.

2. A bull.

3. Crete.

4. Minos.

5. Minos and Rhadamanthus.

6. Daedalus.

7. A large and confusing maze.

8. Two pairs of wings made of feathers fastened to a framework with wax.

9. To help Daedalus and his son Icarus escape from the Labyrinth.

10. To find his sister Europa. Unsuccessfully.

11. By killing a serpent [the son of Mars].

12. The introduction of the alphabet.

13. They were changed into serpents.

14. Laius, that his son would kill him; Oedipus, that he would kill his father. Oedipus tried to avoid this fate by leaving Polybus of Corinth, whom he supposed to be his father, and going to Thebes, where he unknowingly killed his father in a quarrel over the right of way on a road near Delphi.

15. "What creature is it that in the morning goes on four feet, at noon on two, and at night on three?"

16. Callisto was loved by Jupiter.

17. She changed her into a bear.

18. Arcas, too, was changed into a bear, and the two of them were placed in the heavens as the constellations of Ursa Major and Ursa Minor.

19. By visiting Phrygia with Mercury, disguised as humble travelers.

20. Baucis and Philemon.

21. Their supplies of food and wine were made everlasting, their house was transformed to a great temple, they were allowed to die at the same moment, and upon their death they were changed into intertwined trees.

22. & 23. With Neptune for the position of patron deity of Athens, and with Arachne in a spinning and weaving contest.

4   Stories of Venus

Venus and Adonis

This story appears to be a Greek misunderstanding of the Babylonian/Phoenician myth of Ishtar/Astarte and Tammuz, whose title Adon, "Lord," was taken by the Greeks to be his name. (The word is the same as the Hebrew *Adonai*, the word substituted for the Name of God when speaking aloud.) Tammuz was the consort of the Mother-Goddess Ishtar, and when he died she followed him to the subterranean realm of the dead. Immediately all reproduction, plant and animal, ceased on earth while Ishtar was held prisoner by her cruel sister-goddess Allatu (or Eresh-Kigal); finally, at the command of the supreme god, she and Tammuz were released. The annual death and resurrection of Tammuz, who appears to be a vegetation god, were mourned and celebrated in Greece and in many parts of the Near East. A very amusing account of two ladies' attendance at the Adonis funeral in Alexandria may be read in Theocritus' *Idyll 15*. Some such belief must lie behind the annual death of the King in pre-Hellenic Greece and in many other parts of the world. It also seems to have influenced the Isis-Osiris myth in Egypt.

In the Greek version of the story, Adonis was born from the bark of a myrrh- or myrtle-tree into which his mother had been metamorphosed. (This origin may identify him with the tree-spirit whose death and resurrection were celebrated in many parts of the world.) Aphrodite rescued the baby, whom she already loved for his great beauty, and took him in a box to Persephone for safe-keeping. Persephone opened the box and fell in love with Adonis herself. Aphrodite traveled to the Lower World to retrieve him, but was herself detained there until Zeus ordained that Adonis (like Persephone herself, in another myth) would spend half of each year on earth and half in the Lower World. His annual death was marked by the staining of the river Adonis at Byblos with the red soil of the Lebanon at the time of the fall rains. It was said that he had been killed by a boar in the mountains and that the river was carrying his blood to the sea.

Cupid and Psyche

This beautiful story is a good example of a literary myth, put together from folk tales rather than true myths, and containing a large measure of allegory. The folk tale aspects are obvious in the Beauty-and-the-Beast themes of the husband who is lost if he is seen and of the jealous sisters, as well as in the apparently impossible tasks set the heroine (cf., for example, *Rumpelstiltskin*). The allegorical note is also clear: e.g. the Beauty of Proserpina is Death.

Because *psyche* means "butterfly" as well as "soul," Psyche is usually depicted, after her apotheosis, as winged with butterfly wings. The original meaning of the word, however, was "breath," and it is most interesting that in the ancient synagogue excavated at Dura-Europos in Syria (which was built during a brief period when representational paintings were used to decorate synagogues), the Breath of God which animates the dry bones in the valley in the vision of Ezekiel is depicted as a perfectly classical Greek Psyche, even to her butterfly wings.

The myth of Cupid and Psyche has been beautifully retold by C. S. Lewis in *Till We Have Faces*. The story is told in the first person by one of the "wicked" jealous sisters, who is made to seem a sympathetic character, only wanting what is best for her sister.

Atalanta and Hippomenes

The requirement that a suitor perform a difficult task or be put to death appears in other myths (e.g. the story of Pelops and Hippodamia, or of Admetus and Alcestis) and is also common in folk tales.

Because in one version of the myth Atalanta gives a suitor a head start and then kills him with a hunting spear if she can catch up with him, it is possible that this story is an echo of a pre-Hellenic ritual in which the Queen annually sacrificed the King if he failed to escape from her. It is difficult otherwise to account for Atalanta's many suitors, since the Greeks did not admire athletic prowess in women.

Either this Atalanta or Atalanta of Arcadia (if in fact the two are not originally one and the same) was also a wrestler: at the funeral games of King Pelias she defeated King Peleus in a wrestling-match.

Pygmalion and Galatea

Pygmalion is a Greek attempt to pronounce the Phoenician name *Pumiyathon*, and the myth probably comes from the time when the Phoenicians ruled Cyprus, perhaps reflecting a ritual in which the King was married to a statue of the goddess. In this connection, it is interesting that Paphus was either the wife or mother of Cinyras, the father of Adonis, and that both Cinyras and Adonis were thought to have been loved by Aphrodite.

Hero and Leander

Like the story of Cupid and Psyche, this story is an example of a late literary myth. Its inventor is not known, but it may have been based on actual events, since it contains little or nothing of the supernatural.

Pyramus and Thisbe

Except for the nature-myth explanation of the color of the mulberry fruit, there is nothing supernatural in this story either. It is late, being first found in Ovid, who says that it is not a well-known story (which may be his way of telling us that it is a tale of his own invention). The romantic setting in exotic Babylon seems to have no particular relevance to the myth. However, though its ancestry may not be ancient, its progeny are many, including not only *Romeo and Juliet* and *West Side Story* but also (in a kind of reverse way) Rostand's *Les Romanesques*, better known in its adaptation as *The Fantasticks*.

PRACTICAL APPLICATIONS

_____ Myths in Literature_____

The title of the G. B. Shaw play from which *My Fair Lady* was taken is *Pygmalion*. In both stories an artist falls in love with his own creation. The fact that in some versions Pygmalion's creation was meant to be a representation of the goddess Venus may have led to the medieval superstition that a statue of Venus will come to life for anyone who kisses it or places a ring on its finger. Two amusing modern interpretations of this bit of medieval mythology are a novel, S. Anstey's *The Marble Venus*, and the Kurt Weil / S. J. Perelman / Ogden Nash musical, *One Touch of Venus*.

The mechanics' play in *A Midsummer Night's Dream* is worth reading in its entirety, both because it is in itself amusing and because it is a mordant parody of the English classical tragedy of Shakespeare's day. A student with a sense of literary style might like to compare it with, say, Studley's translation of Seneca's *Agamemnon*.

_____ Specific Literary References_____

1. The hunter who was loved by Venus. [This is from Bion's *Lament for Adonis*, a literary version of the hymns which were sung at the

annual death of Adonis/Tammuz in the places where he was worshipped.]

2. Eros/Cupid is usually depicted in literature and the plastic arts as armed with the bow and arrow.

3. From the story of Hippomenes and Atalanta.

4. A reference to the story of Pygmalion and Galatea.

5. & 6. References to the story of Hero and Leander.

7. *Astoreth, Ashtoreth, Astarte,* and *Ishtar* are all versions of the name of the near-eastern goddess whom the Greeks knew as *Aphrodite.*

8. Ignore the promptings of love; a frequent metaphor in modern literature.

9. Cupid is called "heart-quelling" because no one, mortal or divine, can resist his power.

10. The reference is to the chink in the wall through which Pyramus and Thisbe spoke with each other. [A student who is fond of P. G. Wodehouse will be able to find many amusing references of this kind in his writings, particularly in the Jeeves/Bertie Wooster stories. Wodehouse knew his classical literature: Bertie and Jeeves themselves are based upon the brainless young man and the clever body-slave of Terence and especially Plautus.]

11. Adonis was both beautiful and devoted to hunting.

_____ Word Study _____

2. Adonis: a handsome or beautiful young man. Psyche: breath, soul, butterfly. *Psychic, psychotic, psychiatrist, psychosomatic,* etc. Zephyr: the west wind, or any soft, gentle breeze, from the Greek name for the west wind.

3. Venus/Aphrodite, Jupiter (or Jove)/Zeus, Diana/Artemis, Cupid/Eros, Neptune/Poseidon.

_____ Questions for Review _____

1. A beautiful young man of Cyprus.

2. She became a huntress to be with him.

3. He was killed by a wild boar.

4. She mourned his death and persuaded Jupiter to allow him to return to earth for six months of each year.

5. Psyche was receiving the devotion which rightfully belonged to her.

6. He was to make her fall in love with some base person.

7. After he wounded himself with one of his own arrows he fell in love with her.

8. Through an oracle which commanded that she be left on a mountaintop to become the bride of an immortal monster. The "monster" was Cupid.

9. That she must never try to look upon his face.

10. The promptings of her jealous sisters.

11. Cupid was forced to abandon her.

12. The sorting of the seeds, the gathering of the golden wool, and the fetching of the Beauty of Proserpina.

13. With the help of the ants. By gathering the wool from the bushes. By visiting the Lower World and persuading its denizens to have pity on her.

14. Yes, at the intercession of Cupid and Jupiter.

15. Because of a prophecy that marriage would be fatal to her.

16. That they defeat her in a foot-race or die.

17. With the help of Aphrodite he arranged to throw three golden apples ahead of her one at a time, in the hope that she would pause to pick them up.

18. Hippomenes forgot to pay his vow to Aphrodite, and Atalanta failed to thank her.

19. He did not trust them.

20. He was enchanted by the beauty of a statue he had made.

21. That his statue might come to life.

22. By the gradual animation, before his eyes, of the statue.

23. Her parents refused to allow her to marry him.

24. Both sets of parents refused to allow their marriage.

25. Upon Hero's signalling with a lantern, Leander would swim across from Abydos to Sestos to be with her.

26. One night when the wind had blown out the lantern Leander drowned.

27. They had arranged to meet at the tomb of King Ninus at night. Thisbe arrived first but was frightened away by a lioness who stained with blood the veil which Thisbe had dropped. Leander, finding the blood-stained veil, assumed that Thisbe had been killed and killed himself. Thisbe, returning and finding him dying, killed herself with his sword.

28. A mythological Queen of Babylon [and the builder of the city. In Greek and Roman mythology she was the daughter of a goddess and herself became a dove upon her death. She is probably a much mythologized version of Queen Sammuramat of Assyria who ruled 810-805 B.C. An interesting report might be written on the conversion of this historical figure into a mythological one].

29. Originally white, it was stained with the blood of Pyramus and Thisbe.

5   Stories of Apollo

Latona

When Latona/Leto, pursued by the jealousy of Juno, sought a place to give birth to her children, only the floating island of Delos was willing to receive her. In gratitude Jupiter had Delos chained to the sea floor. Apollo and Diana are often called *Delius* and *Delia* from their birthplace; they are also sometimes called *Phoebus* and *Phoebe*, "shining."

Hyacinthus

The tell-tale *nth* in Hyacynthus' name (like that in *Corinth* or *labyrinth*) reveals that we have here a pre-Greek word. It is thought that he was originally a dying and resurrected god of vegetation, like Tammuz/Adonis, worshipped at Amyclae in Lacedaemon. If this is so, the story of his death at the hands of Apollo perhaps echoes the replacement of his worship by that of the Hellenic god. "Casting a quoit" is more familiarly "hurling a discus." It is interesting to see how many persons in classical mythology are killed by stray discuses.

Apollo and Marpessa

Idas, along with his brother Lynceus, was one of the Argonauts. He also took part in the Calydonian Boar Hunt (Meleager was married to Cleopatra, daughter of Idas and Marpessa). It was Idas who killed Castor for having kidnapped two of his female cousins.

Phaëthon and Aesculapius

In the usual versions of the story, Phaëthon is the son, not of Apollo, but of Helios, son of Hyperion and Thea and god of the sun. Helios is later identified with Apollo. Amber was at one time called the "tears of the poplar."

Just as the Central American natives at first imagined that the mounted Spaniards were a new kind of animal, so some suppose that the idea of the Centaur was born of the first appearance in primitive Greece of a mounted man. It is certain that in historic times, at any rate, the Thessalians were known for their horsemanship. The Centaurs were thought of as wild and uncivilized, only half human in their nature as well as in their appearance. They were thought to have little tolerance for alcohol, of which, nevertheless, they were very fond.

Chiron ("Physician") was the tutor of many other heroes besides Aesculapius. Among them were Hercules, Jason, Castor, Pollux, and Achilles.

The mother of Aesculapius (Asclepius to the Greeks) also had a human lover, Ischys. Apollo's raven, at that time a white bird, reported her infidelity to him and was punished by being turned black. Apollo confided in his sister Artemis, who killed Coronis and Ischys with her arrows. Apollo snatched the unborn Asclepius from the funeral pyre and entrusted him to Chiron. According to another story, Coronis exposed the newborn baby on a hilltop near Epidaurus where he was suckled by a wild goat; he was later trained by Chiron.

He married Epione ("Soother"), by whom he was the father of Machaon and Podalirius, the Greeks' physicians at the Trojan War. The rest of their children are personifications and have no mythology, though they were worshipped along with Epione at Asclepius' shrines. They were four daughters, Hygieia ("Health," *Salus* to the Romans), Panacea ("Cure-All"), Iaso ("Healing"), and Aceso ("Cure"), and a son Telesphorus ("Recovery").

The shrines of Asclepius, the most famous of which was at Epidaurus (the remains are among the most interesting of archaeological sites), were in effect sanatoria, with medicinal baths, exercise grounds, and dormitories. Cures were effected by incubation, the practice of sleeping in the temple of the god. Asclepius would appear to the patient in his dreams and heal him or prescribe a remedy. Those who were cured paid for testimonial inscriptions. Many of these have been found at Epidaurus and make very interesting reading. Most of the cures are common sense (e.g. the god tells a man suffering from obesity to eat less), but some seem miraculous (e.g. the restoration of the sight of a man whose eyes had been put out by his falling on the spikes of a fence). One rather odd testimony tells of a barren lady whose only request to the god was that she should become pregnant. He questioned her carefully to make sure that that was all she wanted and she insisted that it was. She returned home, conceived, and remained pregnant for nine years without giving birth, upon which she returned to Epidaurus for relief. The god's first words to her when he appeared in her dream were, "I thought you'd be back."

For the most part, however, the god shows real sympathy with the sufferers and a charming benevolence. A small boy who had been provided by his father with a large sum in gold to offer to the god in exchange for a cure was so won over by the god's kindliness that he impulsively offered him his toys instead, an offering which Asclepius gravely accepted as being more valuable than the gold.

Because of the practice of incubation Asclepius was actually "seen" by more mortals than most gods. His statues show him as looking rather like Zeus, but with a much friendlier expression. The close personal relationship he established with his patients made him an object of more personal devotion than the other gods. His cult was one of the few serious rivals to Christianity, actually reaching its height in the Fourth Century of our era, when nearly all the other pagan gods were fading into insignificance.

His animals are the dog and the serpent, especially the latter, probably because of its reputed powers of regeneration. (The ancients thought that when a snake shed its skin it regained its youth.) He is often depicted with a staff around which a snake is twined, a symbol still used by doctors although, by confusion with the caduceus, there are now two snakes. He also occasionally appears in the form of a serpent, and usually traveled in that form when setting out to found a new shrine/sanatorium. When Rome was afflicted by a plague in 293 B.C., consultation of the Sibylline Books (three rolls bought by Tarquin the Proud from the Sibyl at Cumae) suggested the importation of a new god. The oracle at Delphi (always friendly to the cult of Asclepius) confirmed that he was the god, and that the Romans should apply to Epidaurus. The priests gave the Romans a snake which they brought to Rome with full honors; but, as the barge was being towed up the Tiber, the snake left it and swam to the island next to the city. It was assumed that the god had chosen this site for his temple. There is still a hospital there (now dedicated to St. Bartholomew).

For material for reports on Asclepius, see Aristophanes' *Plutus*, Lucian's *Alexander, the False Prophet*, and *Asclepius*, by E.J. and L. Edelstein, which contains the dedicatory inscriptions.

The Shepherd of King Admetus

Apollo's punishment reflects the human penalty for murder in Greek times, banishment from one's native city. Admetus was one of the Argonauts and also took part in the Calydonian Boar Hunt.

Admetus and Alcestis

In one version of the story, Apollo persuaded the Fates to allow someone else to die in Admetus' place by getting them drunk. He did this by appearing before them disguised as Hermes and carrying a jar of very strong wine which he said was a magic potion he was bringing to Aphrodite at her urgent request. It was the drink which kept her always young and beautiful. Eager to be young and beautiful themselves (they are always depicted as withered crones), they persuaded him to let them drink it. This story is beautifully retold by Thorton Wilder in his *Alcestiad*, two short plays whose action precedes that of Euripides' *Alcestis*.

Athletic Games

There were altogether four sets of panhellenic (international) games. In order of importance, they were: *the Olympic Games*, founded in honor of Zeus in 776 B.C. and held every four years at Olympia; *the Pythian*, founded in honor of Apollo to commemorate his slaying of Python, held at Delphi in the third year of each Olympiad; *the Nemean*, founded in 573 B.C, in honor of Zeus to commemorate Hercules' slaying of the Nemean Lion and held in Nemea in the second and in the fourth year of each Olympiad; and *the Isthmian*, founded in 581 B.C. in honor of Poseidon to commemorate Theseus' killing of Sinis, and held at Corinth every other year. (Sinis was a bandit king who killed all strangers by bending down two pine trees, tying his victim to them, then releasing the trees so that they tore the man in two.) The crown at the Isthmian Games was of parsley, like that at the Nemean. The Isthmian games, while lacking in prestige, were popular, since Corinth was the pleasure city of the Greek world and there were more festivities and amusements at its games.

All who could prove their descent from Hellen, the hero-ancestor of the Greeks, were welcome at the games, though the Spartans refused to attend the Olympic Games after they were reorganized to include other contests than those of running and wrestling. The place of the Spartans was taken by the Greeks of Magna Graecia (Sicily and Italy). Earlier the Spartans had taken most of the prizes and had on one occasion demonstrated their training by rising as one man when they saw an old man trying in vain to find a seat. Before 582 the Pythian games had consisted of contests in instrumental music, singing, drama, and prose and verse recitation. Even after the athletic contests were added, these remained the most important events.

Some books which might prove useful for a report on the games: E. N. Gardner, *Athletics of the Ancient World*, F. A. Wright, *Greek Athletics*, C. Alexander, *Greek Athletics*, and C. A. Forbes, *Greek Physical Education*.

PRACTICAL APPLICATIONS

_____ Specific Literary References _____

1. Phaëthon as the symbol of a brilliant but brief career.

2. The reference is to Phaëthon's brief career as a charioteer.

3. Admetus' wife Alcestis, brought back from the dead.

4. Apollo, with his lyre, is the god of music.

5. The rustics who were turned into frogs for refusing Latona and her twin children, Apollo and Diana, a drink of water.

6. Phaëthon as a metaphor for those who endanger others by their own ambitions.

7. Hercules speaks in Browning's translation of Euripedes' _Alcestis_.

8. A reference to the story of Phaëthon.

_____ Word Study _____

1. The flower sprang from the blood of Hyacinthus, a youth beloved of Apollo. The Iris.

2. An open automobile or carriage with no side-pieces beside or in front of the seats, and hence easy to fall out of, jocularly so named because of the fall of Phaëthon.

   A large non-venomous constricting snake, the reticulated python, the bi-colored rock python (from the great grey-green greasy Limpopo river, to quote Kipling's modern myth), or the Indian python. The reticulated python is the largest of all snakes, attaining a length of thirty feet or more. The art of medicine.

4. Chiron was the wise old medicine-man of the Centaurs, not wild and uncivilized like the others. He was of divine parentage, being the son of Cronus and Philyra, a daughter of Oceanus and Tethys.

5. Latona/Leto, Juno/Hera, Diana/Artemis, Neptune/Poseidon, Jupiter/Zeus.

_____ Questions for Review _____

1. A daughter of the Titans [Coeus and Phoebe] who became by Zeus the mother of Apollo and Artemis.

2. Apollo: the sun, vocal and instrumental music, light, and health. Artemis: the moon, hunting [wild beasts, light, virginity, and childbirth].

3. Hera/Juno.

4. By metamorphosing them into frogs.

5. Hyacinthus.

6. That of Zephyrus.

7. Marpessa.

8. Idas.

9. Phaëthon and Aesculapius/Asclepius.

10. To prove his parentage to his playmates by driving the chariot of the sun.

11. His father swore to grant his wish before he knew what it would be. He was cast to the earth by a thunderbolt.

12. By the Centaur Chiron.

13. Medicine.

14. He was killed by a thunderbolt.

15. He slew the Cyclopes who had forged the thunderbolt.

16. & 17. He banished him from Olympus to be a slave of King Admetus.

18. He was fated to die young [because he had not sacrificed to Artemis at his wedding].

19. She offered to die and give the rest of her years of life to her husband.

20. By Hercules' defeat of Death [or Hades].

21. Python.

22. The Pythian Games.

23. The Olympic Games, the Nemean Games, and the Isthmian Games, to name the panhellenic games. [In addition most cities had local games of their own].

6   Stories of Diana

Endymion

There were two heroes of this name or two myths about this hero, differing widely in locale and circumstances. He is either the shepherd of Mt. Latmos in Caria or the King of Elis in the Peloponnesus, the country where the Olympic Games were held. In the usual version of the first story and in all versions of the second, it is not Diana but Luna (Greek *Selene*), goddess of the moon and daughter of Hyperion and Thea, who loves him. She was later identified with Diana/Artemis.

In the second story Selene's love for Endymion was not so chaste. In fact she bore him fifty daughters, thought to represent the fifty lunar months of an Olympiad. Endymion began the Olympic Games by having his three sons run a footrace to see which one would inherit his kingdom.

Orion

The story of Orion is the earliest of the star-myths. Already in Homer he appears as a constellation with his dog Sirius. He was thought to be the builder of the huge mole at Messena and also to have created the promontory of Pelorum, both in Sicily. His wife Side was killed by Hera for having compared herself to her in beauty. He then wooed Merope, daughter of Oenopion of Chios, the son of Dionysus and Ariadne. Oenopion blinded him in his sleep. Hearing that Eos could heal him, he waded to Lemnos (he was able to walk through the sea either because of his size or because his father was Poseidon), where Hephaestus provided him with a guide to the place where the dawn arose. When Eos looked upon him his sight was restored. From this point his story assumes four different forms. The first is told in the text. According to the second, Eos fell in love with him and carried him off to Delos where he was killed by Artemis because the gods disapproved of the match. In the third he was killed by Artemis in Crete because he challenged her to a discus-throwing contest. In the fourth Gaea sent a scorpion to kill him because he boasted that he would kill all the animals in Crete. According to this last story it was while attempting to restore Orion to life that Asclepius was killed by Zeus' thunderbolt.

The story of Orion's pursuit of the Pleiades is probably derived from the positions of their constellations in the sky. Only six Pleiades are visible; the seventh, Merope, conceals herself from shame at having married a mortal, Sisyphus. Of the others, three had children by Zeus, two by Poseidon, and one by Ares. The story of their transformation into doves may come from a verbal confusion: *peleiades* means "doves" in Greek.

Niobe

There are problems about the geographical location of this myth. Amphion was a Theban hero and the tombs of Niobe's children were shown at Thebes, but the dripping rock into which Niobe was changed was on Mt. Sipylus in Lydia. Some writers say that she returned to her girlhood home before her metamorphosis.

Amphion was one of the great poet-musicians of myth. Like Orpheus, he was able to move stones with his music; in this way he built the walls of Thebes.

Meleager

The Calydonian Boar Hunt was one of the three great occasions at which all the heroes of the generation before the Trojan War gathered, the other two being the voyage of the Argonauts and the funeral games of King Pelias. Meleager and Atalanta were themselves among the Argonauts (some accounts say that Jason had persuaded Atalanta not to join his expedition), and Atalanta wrestled at the funeral games and defeated Peleus. Among those present at the boar hunt were Admetus, Jason, Idas, Castor, Pollux, Nestor, Theseus, and Telamon (father of Ajax). Although Meleager has not as many stories about him as some of the other heroes, he was one of the bravest. His was the only shade in the Lower World which did not retreat from Hercules on his visits there.

The idea that a person's life or soul may inhabit a separate object, as Meleager's does the log, is common in folk tales and is the object of wide-spread belief today, even in modern Greece.

PRACTICAL APPLICATIONS

_____ Specific Literary References _____

1. The reference is to Endymion's eternal sleep.

2. All Niobe's children were slain by Apollo and Artemis.

3. A reference to another version of the Endymion myth in which he is allowed to wake when the moon-goddess visits him.

4. Niobe's daughters were killed by Artemis.

5. Niobe wept so much that she was turned into a fountain [a rock from which a stream gushed].

6. Swinburne is describing Atalanta at the Calydonian Boar Hunt.

7. Tennyson refers to the constellation named for Orion.

8. The reference is to yet another version of the myth, one in which Endymion loses his eyesight, goes mad, and wanders the world, in punishment for having attracted the love of the moon goddess.

_____ Word Study _____

1. Diana/Artemis, Vulcan/Hephaestus, Venus/Aphrodite, Jupiter (or Jove)/Zeus, Latona/Leto.

3. *Orion* was the Nimrod of Greek myth. *Niobe* wasted away in her grief for her children.

_____ Questions for Review _____

1. Yes, with Endymion. [She may also have been in love with Orion and with Hippolytus (Theseus' son)].

2. Death or eternal sleep.

3. Sleep.

4. He was vain of his appearance and of his ability as a hunter.

5. Artemis was tricked by Apollo into shooting at a mark far out to sea, which proved to be Orion's head.

6. In the sky as a constellation pursuing the Pleiades and pursued by the Scorpion.

7. Seven daughters of Atlas and Pleione, daughter of Oceanus and Tethys.

8. By boasting of her superiority to Latona, particularly in the number of her children.

9. Her children, Apollo and Diana.

10. They were killed by the arrows of Apollo.

11. Niobe was still boastful.

12. She was turned into a rock flowing with water.

13. A famous huntress.

14. King Oeneus had forgotten to sacrifice to Diana.

15. Son of Oeneus and Althea.

16. That she heard the Fates saying that he would die as soon as a certain log on the hearth was consumed.

17. He invited all the heroes of Greece to a great boar hunt.

18. All the heroes and Atalanta, also Meleager's two uncles, his mother's brothers.

19. They resented his presenting the spoils of the boar to Atalanta.

20. Meleager killed his uncles.

21. By burning the log which contained his life.

22. She committed suicide when she realized what she had done.

7   Gods of Nature

The Earth

To the early Greeks the actual center of the disk of the earth was Delphi. This was discovered by Zeus when he arranged to have eagles simultaneously released at the eastern and western edges of the earth, and they met directly over Delphi. Hence a sacred stone preserved at Delphi was called the *omphalos* ("navel"). The omphalos is depicted either with a serpent (Python) coiled around it or as draped with a network of unspun fillets of wool (white wool fillets were sacred to Apollo). The true omphalos was kept in the inner shrine of Apollo's temple. A white marble replica, carved with the wool network and flanked by two eagles of gold, stood before the temple. At the end of the second century of our era the Roman Emperor Septimius Severus brought the omphalos to Rome to symbolize the fact that Rome was now the center of the universe. The base which he built for it may still be seen near his Arch in the Roman Forum.

Throughout most of historical times educated Greeks thought or knew that the earth was not flat. In the late sixth century B.C. the Pythagoreans proposed the theory that it was spherical and in the fourth century Aristotle proved it. In the third century B.C. Eratosthenes, a professor at the university (the *Museum*) at Alexandria and librarian of the great library there, calculated its circumference with remarkable accuracy by using shadow-sticks. His minor error arose from the fact that his sticks were not placed due north and south of each other. This same scholar also calculated almost correctly the size and distance of the sun and moon. Eratosthenes was versatile, the Leonardo di Vinci of his day. He was jokingly nicknamed *Beta* ("Number Two") by his colleagues because of all those at the Museum he was the second best literary critic, grammarian, mathematician, geometrician, astronomer, geographer, philosopher, and poet — Number Two in every field. He was interested in mythology and wrote works on the exploits of Hermes and on the constellations and their myths.

In the IVth Century other philosophers suggested that the earth revolved on its axis and in the IIId Century that it revolved around the sun, but these assertions were not universally accepted.

Though it was placed in the far north, the land of the Hyperboreans was thought to be warm because it was located beyond the source of the north wind (*hyper*, "above" or "beyond" in Greek).

The ancients tended to identify as "Ethiopian" any dark-skinned people (the word means "burnt-faced"). Hence Ethiopia was located by various writers anywhere from Nubia to India, including the mouth of the

Tigris and Euphrates. Memnon, son of Eos by Tithonus and the only black we know of to fight in the Trojan War, was usually called Ethiopian.

In the most primitive stories Helios floats back from west to east during the night along the stream of Ocean in a large golden bowl.

Gods of the Earth

We know next to nothing about the old Roman goddess Ceres. At the official level her worship was totally displaced by that of Demeter, to whom the Romans gave her name. In 496 B.C. the Sibylline Books, consulted because of a drought, ordered the introduction of the worship of Demeter from her shrine at Eleusis, along with that of Kore ("Maiden," the usual name for Persephone) and Dionysus. Although the three divinities were given the Latin names of Ceres, Libera, and Liber, their temple (on a spur of the Aventine Hill) was built in the Greek style by Greek architects, and their worship was carried out in the Greek language by women of Greek descent. At Eleusis were celebrated the famous Eleusinian Mysteries, a ritual celebration of the death and rebirth of the grain, which also promised immortal life after death to its initiates.

Dionysus plays a part not only in the Eleusinian mysteries but also in the Orphic religion, and he also has a mystery cult of his own. These mystery religions resemble Christianity in many ways. They are confined to their initiates, have sacraments of initiation and communion with the god, have daily and annually recurring rituals in his honor and in commemoration of events of his life, enforce on their members a moral code, and promise an eternal life after death. They are most interesting and might well form the subjects of reports by your students.

Bacchus' triumphant progress through the world (a myth which probably grew from the rapid spread of his worship) was in a riotous company called a *thiasus*. It consisted of himself and his bride Ariadne, in a chariot drawn by panthers or leopards, and a retinue of Silenus and satyrs, hermaphrodites (strange creatures half-man, half-woman), centaurs, and the maenads. This scene is depicted often in ancient art and literature (for example in Catullus 64).

The real activities of the human maenads were even wilder. Women in the dionysiac ecstasy left their homes and occupations and roamed through the forests, whirling in wild dances, brandishing thyrsi and torches, and seizing wild animals which they dismembered, eating the bloody pieces raw. By this so-called *omophagy* (eating of raw flesh") they believed that they were devouring the body of the god and becoming one with him.

In its later development the religion became less wild, though as late as 186 B.C. the Bacchanalia in Italy had to be put down by a decree of the

Senate. Even in its milder form the religion was still orgiastic and ecstatic, but as its rituals were confined to its initiates not much is known about them. The decorations of the cryptoporticus in the House of the Crypto-porticus and of the mystic oecus in the Villa of the Mysteries, both at Pompeii, have defied definitive interpretation. However, the suggestion that the soul of the worshipper, in the guise of Ariadne, weds the god has gained wide acceptance. The wallpaintings from the Villa of the Mysteries would make an interesting subject for a report.

It is only by accident that Pan's name comes to mean "all." It is actually a variant of *Paon* ("Feeder" of flocks), but in the nominative singular it is spelled the same as the adjective meaning "all" in its neuter form. Because of this coincidence later antiquity came to think of him as a universal god. "Panic fear" was probably attributed to him as the god who causes stampedes in herds, which were felt to be akin to the sudden panic of armies in battle. He could be a dangerous god. In Greece it was felt that it was not safe to be active and noisy at midday, as that was when Pan took his siesta and would resent being disturbed. This feeling about the dangers of noontime activity is still current in Greece.

The satyrs come into mythology from folklore. Mischievous prankish beings, they resemble the fays or fairies of English tales.

The Oceanids and the Nereids, as their names imply, were the daughters of Oceanus and of Nereus.

Gods of the Dawn, Dusk, and Air

Eos is a daughter of the Titans Hyperion and Thea and a sister of Helius and Selene. She was by the Titan Astraeus (a son of Crius and Eurybia, a daughter of Pontus) the mother of Boreas, Zephyrus, and Notus.

In Homer Aeolus is a mortal who has been entrusted by Zeus with the care of the winds. In Virgil he is a minor god. The Latin names of the winds are Boreas/Aquilo, Zephyrus/Favonius, Notus/Auster and Eurus/Volturnus. But although the Romans personified the winds, they gave them no mythology. Latin writers tended to use the Greek names in mythological contexts.

Gods of the Waters

Nereus was the son of Pontus, a son of Gaea. His brother Phorcys and sister Ceto, also sea-gods, were the parents of the Gray Sisters, the Gorgons, Ladon (the serpent who guarded the Apples of the Hesperides), and Thoosa, a nymph who became by her father the mother of the Sirens and Scylla.

Nereus' daughter Galatea was loved by Acis (son of Faunus and a river-nymph) and by the Cyclops Polyphemus. She naturally preferred Acis to the grotesque Polyphemus, so Polyphemus eliminated his rival by crushing him under a huge boulder. This for some reason failed to win Galatea's love. She changed the blood of her beloved to the River Acis which gushes from under a rock near Mt. Etna in Sicily. An amusing account of Polyphemus' sprucing himself up and then wooing the sophisticated Galatea with rustic compliments is given in Ovid's *Metamorphoses*, Book XIII.

The three Sirens were at first of human form and were the playmates of Persephone. When Persephone was kidnapped by Hades, the Sirens were turned into half-birds, half-women so that they could search the world for her. Later they competed with the Muses in song. When they lost the contest they were deprived of their wings. They were also doomed to die if anyone hearing their song was unmoved. When Orpheus passed in the *Argo* and surpassed their song with his own, they plunged into the sea and were changed into rocks. Their names were either Molpe, Aglaopheme, and Thelxiepeia or Ligeia, Leucosia, and Parthenope. Belief in the Sirens persisted into Christian times and they are often represented in the carvings of medieval churches. The Lorelei of the Rhine is an obvious descendant of the Sirens.

Another god of the sea, worshipped especially by fisherman, was Glaucus, who was originally a mortal and a fisherman himself. Having laid his catch upon the grass one day, he was amazed to see that the fish came back to life and returned to the sea. He ate some of the herb upon which they had been lying and immediately felt a great longing to jump into the sea. When he had done this Oceanus and Tethys transformed him into a merman. In this form he fell in love with the lovely Scylla. When she would have nothing to do with him, he appealed to the sorceress Circe for help. Unfortunately Circe fell in love with him and, when he scorned her, avenged herself by pouring a magic potion into the cove where Scylla used to bathe. It was this poison which changed the lower part of Scylla's body so that she became a monster. Glaucus thereafter annually made the rounds of all the Mediterranean shores, delivering prophecies and bewailing the fact that the herb he had eaten had made him immortal, so that he could not forget Scylla in death.

Charybdis is evidently an attempt to explain a large whirlpool. It has been thought that the original of the monstrous Scylla was some early mariner's first sight of a large Atlantic squid or octopus.

PRACTICAL APPLICATIONS

_____ Reference to Mythology in Literaturee _____

1. Bacchus, the god of wine, wandered the world with his attendants.

2. Pan, who had the beard, ears, tail, and legs of a goat, played the pan-pipes.

3. The trident (actually a gaff used by ancient Greek fishermen) was Neptune's chief attribute. He used it both for stirring up the sea and for striking the earth in earthquakes.

4. & 5. Ceres/Demeter was goddess of the bounteous harvest.

6. Eos (Aurora) was goddess of the dawn.

7. A dryad was a tree nymph.

8. The Hesperides, daughters of Hesper (or of his daughter Hesperis and Atlas), guarded in their garden the tree bearing the golden apples which Gaea had given to Juno as a wedding present.

9. An oread was a mountain nymph.

10. Silenus, chief of the Satyrs, is represented as fat and drunken.

11. Boreas is an autonomasia for "winter."

12. Bacchus in his travels was accompanied by satyrs and bacchantes, women maddened by religious fervor.

13. Aeolus had been appointed by Jupiter to rule the winds.

14. The west wind was for the Romans the wind of spring.

15. Proteus rose from the sea every day at noon; it was then that he could be caught. Triton is usually depicted as playing on a seaweed-wrapped conch shell.

_____ Word Study _____

1. _Panic_: from Pan, god of stampedes and of lonely places. _Cereal_: from Ceres, goddess of grain. _Boreal_: from Boreas, the north wind. _Auroral_: from Aurora, goddess of the dawn, called by Homer "rosy-fingered" or "rosy-toed;" the word means "rosy-digited." _Aurora borealis_: so called because it appears in the north and resembles the dawn. _Zephyr_: from Zephyrus, the west wind. _Protean_: from Proteus, the Old Man of the Sea, who could change his shape. _Bacchic_: from Bacchus, god of wine and ecstasy. _Siren_: jocularly from the

Sirens, who lured mariners onto the rocks with their song.

2. Jupiter/Zeus, Ceres/Demeter, Neptune/Poseidon, Bacchus/ Dionysus, Aurora/Eos. Thyrsus.

3. "Between a rock and a hard place," "Between the Devil and the deep blue sea." He is fat and/or jovial and/or a drunkard. She is a *femme fatale*, capable of heartlessly luring men to their deaths or worse. A musical instrument consisting of a box with thin strings stretched over it, tuned so that it is played by the movement of air. Aeolian harps were popular in the Eighteenth Century.

4. They have in common their prankish maliciousness.

5. No. They have in common only their beauty and the fact that the Nymphalidae, unlike most insects, appear to have only four limbs. The vagaries of biologists' nomenclature is revealed by their naming one of the Nymphalidae sub-families Satyrinae.

_____ Questions for Review _____ _____

1. At first, that it was round and flat, with Delphi in the center and the River Oceanus flowing around its edge. [From the IVth Century B.C. onward their notion was the same as ours except that they knew nothing about the western, and little about the southern, hemisphere.]

2. Cultivated plants, particularly wheat.

3. Persephone/Proserpina [more often worshipped as Kore/Libera].

4. Joyous and kindly [occasionally irresponsible and cruel].

5. Wine, the bounty of vegetation, fertility, ecstatic religion.

6. As a beautiful somewhat effeminate youth, wreathed with grapevine or ivy, carrying the Thyrsus. He often rides in a chariot drawn by leopards [or panthers, and is accompanied by his thiasus].

7. The god of flocks and herdsmen, also of nature. He was represented as a hook-nosed man with the beard, ears, and lower legs of a goat; he carries the pan-pipes.

8. The Satyrs.

9. Silenus.

10. Dryads (or hamadryads), Oceanids, Nereids, naiads, and oreads.

11. Aurora (Eos).

12. The morning star. The evening star. The daughters of Hesper (or of his daughter Hesperis and Atlas).

13. Aeolus. Boreas [Aquilo] and Zephyrus [Favonius].

14. The Titans Oceanus and Tethys.

15. He was both their nephew (son of their brother Cronus) and their grandson-in-law (husband of their granddaughter Amphitrite).

16. A son of Pontus, son of Gaea, and husband of Doris, a daughter of Oceanus and Tethys.

17. Nereids.

18. A merman, son of Neptune and Amphitrite, and herald and trumpeter for his father. The Old Man of the Sea, hersdman of Neptune's flocks, the seals, and a prophet. He was forced to prophesy for anyone who could cling to him while he metamorphosed himself into various shapes.

19. Three nymphs [daughters of Nereus and Thoosa] who sang sweet songs to lure mariners onto the rocks. Two monsters who guarded a strait; Scylla had six long necks with dogs' heads, with which she would snatch six mariners from any passing ship; Charybdis, by drinking in and spewing forth the waters of the sea, created a huge whirlpool on the other side.

8   Stories of the Gods of Nature

Ceres, Proserpina, and Pluto

Dis is the Latin name for the Greek Hades. *Pluto* is his Greek nickname. Both *Dis* and *Pluto* mean "the wealthy one." There is also a god strictly of wealth, called Plutus, who is a son of Demeter. He was nursed by Tyche ("Good Luck") and Irene ("Peace"). He was blinded by Zeus, which is why he always grants riches to the wrong people.

Jupiter's disposing of Proserpina's hand in marriage is understandable, since he was her father. Proserpina is more properly the goddess of the grain itself, coming up out of the ground in spring and put into underground granaries in the fall.

Demeter had many adventures as she wandered the earth in grief for her lost daughter. Arriving in disguise at Eleusis, she was kindly received by King Celeus and comforted her sorrow by becoming the nurse of his infant son Demophoon. Wishing to make the child immortal she nightly anointed him with ambrosia, then placed him in the fire to burn away his mortality. But his mother Metanira came upon them one night and screamed at the sight of her child burning (as she thought). The spell was broken and the baby died in the flames. Demeter wrathfully resumed her own form and demanded that the Eleusinians build her a temple and that Celeus and Metanira give her their other son, Triptolemus, to be its priest. Triptolemus became Demeter's ambassador. He traveled the world in a chariot drawn by serpents and taught the cultivation of grain to mankind. It was to him that Demeter revealed the sacred mysteries that were celebrated at Eleusis.

Bacchus

Persephone is, in a very strange way, also the mother of Bacchus (according at least to the Orphic mysteries). She became by Zeus the mother of Zagreus, whom Zeus intended to make his successor as ruler of the universe. But jealous Hera told the Titans of this plan and they tore the child to pieces and ate them. Zeus saved Zagreus' heart, which he devoured. He then chose Semele, one of Cadmus' daughters, as the new mother of the child, who was thus to be reborn. Semele's jealous sisters made her doubt whether her handsome lover was really the god. She persuaded him to swear by Styx to grant her wish and then asked to see him as he appeared to his fellow gods. When he granted her wish, she burst into flames at the sight and was consumed. However, Zeus snatched the unborn child from the ashes and placed it in his thigh until it was time for it to be born. The baby was then given to Semele's sister Ino to nurse. Ino was eventually punished by Hera by the madness of her husband Athamas.

The implacable cruelty of Dionysus toward those who would not receive his cult is illustrated by the stories of Pentheus, the Minyades, and Lycurgus. The story of Pentheus has been told in the comments on *Oedipus* in Lesson 3. When the rest of the women of Boeotia were wandering the hills in Bacchic frenzy, the Minyades, daughters of Minyas, King of Orchomenus, stayed at home weaving. The god, appearing in the shape of a beautiful maiden, warned them to accept the cult. When they would not listen, he assumed in turn the forms of a bull, a lion, and a panther. He then turned their weaving into grapevines and made wine and milk flow from the loom-beam. Terrified, they drew lots as to which of them should make the sacrifice. The lot fell upon Leucippe, who tore her own son to pieces in the Bacchic frenzy. Then, as the Minyades wandered the hills, they were turned into bats.

The story of Lycurgus is even more gruesome. He was a Thracian king who persecuted the child Dionysus and forced him to take shelter with Thetis beneath the sea. On his return Dionysus drove the king mad so that he cut off the arms and legs of his own son under the delusion that he was pruning a grapevine. The god then cursed his land with barrenness until Lycurgus' own people led him out to Mt. Pangaeus, where Dionysus had him torn to pieces by wild horses. For this recurring theme of dismemberment, compare the practice of omophagy, mentioned previously.

Midas

Midas may originally have been a historical figure: his name, in the form *Mita*, is Phrygian and was borne by at least one historical Phrygian king.

The ancients did not have the musical instrument we call a "flute." Pan's instrument is properly a syrinx or pan-pipes, pipes of graduated size bound together. Another instrument often called a flute was the *aulos*, a shawm or reed instrument more like an oboe in its sound. The aulos was invented by Minerva, who played it happily until she caught sight of her reflection in a pool. The sight of her distended cheeks disgusted her so much that she threw the instrument away. It was picked up by a satyr called Marsyas, who became so proficient on it that he challenged Apollo to a musical contest, the winner being allowed to do as he liked with the loser. When Marsyas lost, Apollo had him flayed alive and hung up his skin, from which flowed thereafter the River Marsyas (in Asia Minor). In some versions of the myth, it was at this contest that Midas was the unfortunate judge.

Io

Juno's jealousy was intensified by the fact that Io had been the first priestess in Juno's temple at Argos. The various water-crossings which were called *Bosporus* ("Oxford" or "Cattle-crossing") were thought to have been named from Io's having crossed them in her wanderings. The name is still used for the straits between the Sea of Marmora and the Black Sea.

By Zeus Io became the mother of Epaphus, whose daughter Libya gave her name to the continent we call Africa (and ultimately to a nation of modern Africa). Libya had by Neptune a child called Belus. This name was a Greek attempt to pronounce Baal, a semitic word for "Lord," and was given in Greek mythology to any eastern king whose name was not known. Belus' sons were Aegyptus, after whom Egypt was named, Danaus, Cepheus, and Phineus of Ethiopia. (These last three appear in myths later in the book.) Io's father Inachus was himself a son of Oceanus and Tethys.

Upon her arrival in Egypt Io became the Egyptian goddess Isis, whose mystery religion included many Greeks and Romans among its worshippers from the ɪᴠth Century B.C. on. The identification is a strange one, since Hathor, not Isis, was the Egyptian cow-goddess. However, it is confirmed by much evidence, including the very interesting wall paintings from the Temple of Isis at Pompeii. These paintings, and indeed the worship of Isis in general, would make good subjects for reports.

Apollo and Daphne

Daphne's other admirer, Leucippus son of Oenomaus, disguised himself as a girl in order to join the group of nymphs who were her playmates. However, Apollo betrayed him to the nymphs, and they killed him.

Apollo and Clytie

This story is a good example of the nature-myth pure and simple. It has no point except to explain the existence of heliotropic plants.

Echo and Narcissus

The story of Echo is late, and may have been invented by Ovid. In his version, Narcissus' parents asked the seer Tiresias if the boy would have a long life, and received the puzzling reply, "Only if he doesn't get to know himself." It is the goddess Nemesis who makes him fall in love with his reflection. The narcissus flower was thought to cause torpor or numbness, like that into which Narcissus fell before he died. The root of the name is seen also in *narcotic.*

Aurora and Tithonus

Another nature-myth, this one explains why the grasshopper (or, in some versions, the cicada) sings to greet the dawn.

Tithonus was the brother of Priam. Aurora's son by him, Memnon, became the King of the Ethiopians, whom he led to Priam's aid in the Trojan War. Because of the vagueness of the ancients about the location of Ethiopia, various monuments of Persia and Egypt were thought to have been erected by, or in honor of, Memnon. The most famous of these was the "vocal Memnon" in Egypt, actually a statue of Amenophis. After it was damaged by an earthquake in 27 B.C. it produced a musical sound when warmed by the sun's first rays. This was supposedly Memnon greeting his mother. Waiting for dawn by the statue was a great tourist attraction until it was repaired and the sounds ceased.

Ceyx and Halcyone

Ceyx was the son of Phosphor, who was the son, by Astraeus, of Aurora.

PRACTICAL APPLICATIONS

_____ Specific Literary References _____

1. The gift of Midas was the golden touch, which would have made him starve amidst riches. It is insane to wish for wealth which brings death with it.

2. The mortal Tithonus was the consort of Eos, goddess of the dawn.

3. Proserpina was gathering flowers when Dis abducted her.

4. Echo is invisible, her body having wasted away in her longing for Narcissus.

5. Ovid describes Narcissus as still narcissistic in the Lower World.

6. Because of the calm granted by Aeolus to the kingfisher Halcyone so that she may hatch her young, any peaceful undisturbed times are called "halcyon days."

7. Proserpina became the consort of Dis, who is depicted as stern and unyielding, only unwillingly.

_____ Word Study _____

1. Dis/Hades (Pluto), Liber/Dionysus (Bacchus), Juno/Hera, Mercury/Hermes, Cupid/Eros, Diana/Artemis, Aurora/Eos.

2. A young cow; a soft conical cap rounded at the point, which usually droops a little forward. (In ancient art it was used to indicate an Asiatic. Because such a cap was given to a manumitted slave among the Romans, it is called a liberty cap and in modern art is sometimes worn by the Goddess of Liberty); pan-pipes; an orange-sized red berry, whose tough skin encloses many seeds, each surrounded by a juice-filled membrane.

3. For a poet to be "crowned with laurel" (the meaning of the word) means that he is the victor in the games of Apollo, and hence the best of poets.

4. An ability to become rich with apparent ease; peaceful, undisturbed times; someone who is powerful because of his wealth.

5. As the name of a nymph who was condemned to be unable to speak except by repeating the words of others; it was the sea across which Io swam in the form of a heifer.

_____ Questions for Review _____

1. Dis and Hades.

2. The Lower World, all beneath the surface of the earth.

3. Persephone/Proserpina (Proserpine).

4. He abducted her by appearing in his chariot from a sudden chasm in the earth and snatching her away.

5. She ceased to care for the crops of earth, and permanent winter came.

6. Her daughter could return if she had not eaten in the realm of Hades.

7. Proserpina had eaten six pomegranate seeds.

8. The annual disappearance and reappearance of the grain.

9. He changed them into dolphins.

10. Pan [or Marsyas] and Apollo.

11. Midas; against Apollo.

12. He gave Midas the ears of an ass.

13. His wish for a golden touch, granted by Silenus, nearly caused him to starve.

14. Daughter of the river-god Inachus [first King of Argos, and herself the first priestess of Hera in her great temple there].

15. By attracting the love of Jupiter.

16. A heifer.

17. Argus.

18. Disguised as a shepherd, he lulled him to sleep by playing on the syrinx and telling him a story.

19. Daphne.

20. By praying to her father, who turned her into a laurel tree.

21. Clytie's.

22. She became a sunflower.

23. She was a nymph whom Juno condemned to be able to speak only by repeating the words of others.

24. Narcissus.

25. He pined away for love of his own image.

26. Immortality.

27. Eternal youth.

28. To consult the oracle in Claros.

29. He was shipwrecked and drowned.

30. She was the goddess of married love.

31. They became kingfishers.

9   Stories of the Underworld

Regions of the Underworld

Lake Avernus, between Cumae and Puteoli (modern Cuma and Pozzuoli) in Italy, fills the deep crater of an extinct volcano; it was thought to be an entrance to the Lower World because of its darkness and depth and because volcanic vapors rise from it and from the land around it. It was, however, only one of several entrances to the dwelling of Hades. The most famous of the others were a cave on Taenarum, the southernmost promontory of the Peloponnesus, and another near Heracleum on the Black Sea.

Styx, the nymph of the river called after her, was the eldest daughter of Oceanus and Tethys. As she was the first of the Titan race to help the Olympians in their battle against the Titans, by bringing her children, Zeal, Force, Strength, and Victory to help, the gods honored her by considering inviolable any oath taken in her name. When a god wished to swear, Iris was sent to bring some of the water of the Styx in a golden cup and the god poured out the water while taking the oath. A god who broke such an oath was required to be dead for a year and then to be in exile for another nine. The Styx flowed into the Lower World from the River Ocean, at a point where the goddess Styx had her palace. A branch of the Styx, the Cocytus, flowed, along with the Phlegethon and the Pyriphlegethon, into the Acheron. Bathing in the Styx granted invulnerability. Charon was the son of Styx and Erebus (Darkness).

Cerberus was the son of the Giant Typhon (who had a hundred serpent heads, a hundred pairs of hands and feet and spoke in the noises of all the animals) and the sea-goddess Echidna, who was half woman, half snake. Their other children included Geryon's two-headed dog Orthus, the Hydra, the Chimera, the sleepless serpent which guarded the Golden Fleece, and the eagle which devoured Prometheus' liver. By Orthus the Chimera also became the mother of the Sphinx and the Nemean Lion. Ugly as Cerberus was, he was almost the pick of the litter.

Pluto's cap of darkness is sometimes called a helmet. It rendered its wearer invisible and had been made by the Cyclopes to help Pluto in the battle of the Olympians against the Titans. *Hades* is properly Pluto's real name. It was not used until very late to refer to the realm he governed which was usually called "the dwelling of Hades." Erebus, the god of Primeval darkness, son of Chaos and brother of Night, gave his name first to the area through which the souls passed on their way to the dwelling of Hades, and then to the whole realm. At first the realm was thought of as undifferentiated with the souls of the dead flitting aimlessly about.

Elysium was originally thought of as lying beyond the Islands of the Blest on the far western shore of the River Ocean — in fact, the place where we Americans now live. Tartarus also was not at first considered a part of Hades' realm, but was below it, as far below as heaven was above. It was surrounded by a wall of iron made by Poseidon and was the prison of Cronus and the defeated Titans, who were later, after their reconciliation with the Olympians, transferred to Elysium. Later both these places became part of the dwelling of Hades, as places of reward and punishment respectively. Souls were assigned to one or the other by the three judges, Minos, Rhadamanthus, and Aeacus (Triptolemus was sometimes added as a fourth).

Christian ideas of Hell have borrowed much from the dwelling of Hades. You might like to have a student report on Dante's *Inferno* or Michelangelo's *Last Judgment* (in the Sistine Chapel of the Vatican).

Chief Figures of Hades

The Furies' real name was *Erinyes*; like Hades, they were given a nick-name (*Eumenides*, "Well-Wishers") to avoid pronouncing their real name and perhaps offending or, worse, summoning them. In the same way the fairies are called "the Little People," "the Good Folk," or (in Ireland) "the Gentry." The Furies carried torches with which they madden those whom they pursue. Their names were Allecto ("Unresting"), Tisiphone ("Murder-Avenger"), and Megaera ("Jealous").

Hecate was a Titaness, a favorite of Zeus and the only one of the Titans left in undisturbed possession of her power. Because she had power under, upon, and above the earth she is thought of as a triple goddess, and her statues are usually of three ladies joined back to back and holding the various symbols of her power (keys, torches, snakes, etc.). She is in some mysterious way identified with Selene, Artemis, and Persephone. The Romans called her *Trivia* ("Three-Way") and made her also a goddess of crossroads ("Trivial" matters are the kind gossiped about at crossroads).

Death and Sleep were the sons of Night. Morpheus, son of Sleep, sends dreams about human beings; his brother Phobetor sends dreams about animals; and their brother Phantasos dreams about inanimate objects.

Dwellers in Tartarus

There are conflicting stories about Tantalus' crimes, but two of them seem especially worthy of the punishment assigned to him in Tartarus. As a son of Zeus and one of the nymphs, he was on visiting terms with the gods, inviting them to dinner and being invited in return. On one of the latter occasions he stole some nectar and ambrosia from the gods' table and served them later to his friends. Later, when the gods were dining at his house, he killed and cooked his son Pelops (throwing away the obviously recognizable head, hands, and feet) and served him in a stew to the gods, in an attempt to find out if the gods were really omniscient. They were and, recognizing the nature of the dish, turned away in horror — all but Demeter, who, being distraught with grief over the loss of Persephone, absent-mindedly ate Pelops' shoulder. The gods found all the other pieces and reassembled and reanimated the boy, giving him a shoulder carved out of ivory to replace the missing part. As a result, all of Pelops' descendants had one very white shoulder. They then transported Tantalus to Tartarus. He could not be killed because he had eaten ambrosia and was hence immortal. Pelops and his sister Niobe then migrated from their father's kingdom in Lydia to Greece: he to the Peloponnesus, which took its name from him, and she to Thebes, where she married Jupiter's son Amphion and had by him her seven sons and seven daughters.

Ixion was King of the Lapiths. A grandson of Ares, he was the brother of Coronis, Asclepius' mother. He, too, was a personal friend of the gods. He was considered to be the first person ever to have killed a kinsman. When he married Dia, he refused to give to her father Deioneus the bridal gifts he had promised. So the next time he visited his father-in-law, Deioneus impounded his horses. Enraged, Ixion invited Deioneus to dinner, but dug a deep pit across the path to his door, filled it with glowing coals and covered it over. Deioneus fell into it and was burned alive. Because of their friendship, Zeus offered to purify Ixion from this hideous blood-guilt. He brought him to heaven for this purpose, but while he was there Ixion dared to attempt to win the love of Hera. Zeus created an image of Hera from clouds, which yielded to Ixion and became by him the mother of the Centaurs, which are often called "cloud-born." Ixion compounded his ingratitude by boasting to his friends of his success with "Hera," thus finally trying his friend Zeus' patience too far.

Ixion's son (or the son of his wife Dia by Zeus) and successor as King of the Lapiths was Pirithous, the friend of Theseus. He was another famous dweller in Tartarus. He and his friend Theseus, after the deaths of their wives, Hippodamia and Phaedra, together resolved that they would each marry a daughter of Zeus and would help each other in this enterprise. Theseus chose Helen, who was still a young child. Together Pirithous and Theseus abducted her and left her with Theseus' mother Aethra at Troezen. To Theseus' horror, Pirithous then revealed that he wished to marry Persephone, wife of the dread Hades. Bound by his promise, Theseus reluctantly joined his friend in a journey to the Lower World. There they were caught and chained to a rock or made to sit in chairs to which their skin grew fast so that they could not rise from them. Pirithous remained imprisoned forever, but Theseus was set free by Hercules on his Twelfth Labor and returned to Troezen to find that Helen had been rescued by her brothers Castor and Pollux.

Sisyphus, the grandfather of Bellerophon, is a figure more out of folk tale than myth. He is the Greek version of the clever trickster who appears in the folklore of so many lands, a remote ancestor of Brer Rabbit. When another trickster, Autolycus, was stealing his cattle, Sisyphus put metal shoes on them with the engraving, "Stolen by Autolycus." In this was he was able to track them down and get them back. Sisyphus built the city of Corinth but then found that it had an inadequate water supply. When Zeus abducted the nymph Aegina (by whom he became the father of Aeacus, father of Peleus), Sisyphus observed that he had taken her to the island which afterward bore her name. Meeting Aegina's father, the River Asopus, who was in search of his daughter, Sisyphus agreed to reveal her whereabouts only if Asopus would create the spring Peirene which ever afterward supplied Corinth with water. Enraged by this betrayal of his secret, Zeus sent Death for Sisyphus, but Sisyphus, expecting him, lay in ambush, seized him, and bound him in chains. While Death was bound, no one on earth could die. Finally Zeus sent Ares to free Death and hand Sisyphus over to him. Sisyphus persuaded Death to let him say goodbye to his wife and whispered to her that she was not to bury his body. In the Lower World he complained to Hades and Persephone of his wife's failure to give him a funeral and got their permission to return to life temporarily to reproach her. Once back on earth he conveniently forgot to return and eventually died of old age. This time when Hades got his hands on him he condemned him to the rock-rolling task so that he could not run away again.

Danaus was the great-great-grandson of Io. He had fifty daughters and his twin brother Aegyptus had fifty sons. Their father Belus gave the kingship of Egypt to Danaus but, fearing assassination by one of his fifty nephews, he fled with his daughters to Argos to the protection of his great-great-grandmother's kinsmen. The fifty sons of Aegyptus pursued them and demanded the hands of the fifty girls in marriage. Danaus agreed but gave each girl a dagger with instructions to kill her husband on the wedding night. Forty-nine of them did so, and also cut off and buried their husband's heads, but the fiftieth, Hypermnestra, who loved her husband Lynceus (not the Argonaut), helped him to escape. He later returned and succeeded Danaus as King of Argos. In some versions the task of the Danaids is to try to fill with water a jar with holes in its bottom.

The only other famous dweller in Tartarus was Tityus, a Giant who attacked Leto and was killed by the arrows of Apollo and Artemis. He was stretched out on a plain, where his body covered nine acres, and two vultures perpetually tore at his liver.

Islands of the Blest

In early times, the Islands of the Blest were thought of as off to the west, in the River Ocean, while Elysium was on its further bank. Certain favored persons were brought to the Islands or to Elysium without ever tasting death. It was later, as the concept of an after-life took shape, that these places were transferred to the Lower World as abodes for the dead rather than the living. The idea of a kind of paradise far out on the Atlantic persisted, however, in folklore, and re-emerges in the Middle Ages as Avalon.

Orpheus and Eurydice

Orpheus is sometimes called the son of Oeagrus, King of Thrace, and Calliope. Followers of the Orphic religion (a mystery religion dating from the vith Century b.c.) claimed him as its founder. He may have been a real person whose life was later mythologized.

Perhaps because of the Orphic religion, Orpheus was a popular figure. He appears frequently in ancient paintings, playing his lyre to an admiring circle of wild animals. The same painting even appears in Christian tombs, perhaps as a representation of the Prince of Peace. The Romans were fond of an entertainment they called an "Orphic spectacle," in which a concert singer performed while trained animals gathered around to listen. At an Orphic spectacle performed during the games which inaugurated the Colosseum, an insufficiently trained bear unfortunately killed and ate the artist.

Orpheus' death may be added to those of the other unfortunates who opposed the worship of Dionysus. It is said that his head was torn off and thrown into the sea where it floated, still singing, to the island of Lesbos where it was buried. Lesbos later was the home of some of the best Greek lyric poets.

PRACTICAL APPLICATIONS

_____ Myths in Literature _____

A very interesting, if somewhat surrealistic, modern treatment of the Orpheus myth may be found in Jean Cocteau's *Orphée* and his film of the same title.

_____ Specific Literary References_____

1. Elysium was the Paradise of the ancients.

2. Orpheus looks back at Eurydice a moment too early, and so loses her again.

3. Sisyphus' stone always rolls back down the mountain just as it almost reaches the top.

4. Cerberus was the serpent-tailed three-headed dog which guarded the entrance to the Dwelling of Hades.

5. Drinking the water of Lethe caused forgetfulness of all past events.

6. Pluto was a name for Hades, King of the Lower World, where all kinds of monsters lurked.

7. Tantalus' punishment included the receding of the water whenever he stooped to drink.

8. The Happy Isles were the Islands of the Blest, in this poem pictured as far to the west on the Atlantic.

9. The River of Woe, one of the rivers of the Lower World.

10. Styx: another river of the Lower World, the one which the souls must cross on their arrival. Charon: their ferryman.

_____ Word Study_____

1. *Lethean*: from *lethe*, the Greek word for "forgetfulness," from which the river took its name. *Elysian*: from Elysium, the Paradise of the ancients. *Hypnotic*: from *hypnos*, the Greek word for "sleep." *Morphine*: from the name of Morpheus, a god of dreams. *Tantalize*: from Tantalus, for whom in Tartarus food and drink were always just out of reach. *Orphic*: a word originally referring to the mystery religion supposedly founded by Orpheus.

3. Dis/Pluto/Hades, Ceres/Demeter, Somnus/Hypnos, Mors/Thanatos, Liber/Bacchus/Dionysus.

4. A Greek coin (worth in vth-Century Athens about $3.00 in buying power); an unattractive weed with sparse dirty-white scentless flowers, usually planted on graves; a musical instrument consisting of a sound-box in the shape of a tortoise-shell, with two arms shaped like curved horns and with a bar between them, over which were stretched seven strings of equal length.

5. To swear an inviolable oath; false dreams; to perform a useless,

never-ending task, like that of the Danaids; a pacifier, like the drugged tidbit Aeneas threw to Cerberus; utter primeval darkness; an unhealthy drowsiness or apathy, from the Greek word for "forgetfulness."

_____ Questions for Review _____

1. The Lower World, the Realm or Dwelling of Hades, Erebus, Orcus, Acheron.

2. Pluto (Hades/Dis).

3. Styx (River of Hatred), Cocytus (River of Wailing), Phlegethon (Flaming) [Pyriphlegethon (Flaming with Fire)], Acheron (River of Woe), Lethe (Forgetfulness).

4. Charon.

5. Cerberus.

6. Acheron, Elysium, Tartarus.

7. Goddesses who avenged certain crimes by pursuing and maddening the criminals.

8. A Titaness, goddess of the Lower World and witchcraft [and of crossroads].

9. Hypnos/Somnus; Thanatos/Mors; Morpheus [Phobetor, Phantasos].

10. By being placed within apparent reach of food and water, which however were withdrawn when he tried to get them, for many crimes [especially for having stolen nectar and ambrosia and for having served his son in a stew to the gods]; by being bound to an everwhirling wheel, for having killed his father-in-law [and for having insulted Hera]; by being made to roll a rock up a mountain side endlessly, for his avarice and fraud [especially for having revealed to Asopus the hiding-place of Zeus and Aegina and for having eluded Death]; by being made to carry water in sieves [or to try to fill a bottomless pot], for having killed their husbands.

11. Pleasant air and light, leisure and idleness.

12. A famous bard of Thrace.

13. She was bitten by a poisonous snake and died.

14. That he be allowed to bring her back to the upper world.

15. That he might, provided he did not look at her until they had arrived.

16. At the last moment Orpheus looked back at her and she was once more lost.

17. By being dismembered by Maenads.

10 Stories of Heroes and Friends

Trials of Perseus

Acrisius was the grandson of Lynceus; Danae was named for her great-great-grandfather.

The Gorgons were the daughters of Phorcys and Ceto. Two of them, Stheno ("Mighty") and Euryale ("Wide-Ranging"), were immortal monsters; Medusa ("Queen") was mortal and was originally a beautiful maiden. Poseidon loved her and she accepted his advances in a temple of the virgin goddess Athena. In revenge for this desecration, Athena made her a monster like her sisters.

The Gray Sisters, who were sisters also of the Gorgons, were born old and gray-haired. Their extreme age explains why they had only one eye and one tooth left among them. (In order to eat they had to take turns using the tooth.) In most versions of the story, Perseus steals the tooth as well as the eye. The names of the Gray Sisters, Pemphredo ("Wasp"), Enyo ("War-Goddess"), and Dino ("Dreadful"), seem inappropriate. Perhaps they were originally bogies of folklore, used for frightening children into being good.

From the neck of Medusa sprang her two children by Poseidon, the winged horse Pegasus and his brother Chrysaor, the father (by the Oceanid Callirhoe) of Geryon and Echidna. The blood which poured from her body was caught by Apollo and given to Asclepius, who used the blood from one vein as a poison which caused disease, and the blood from another to restore the dead to life. When Perseus carried the head over the sands of the desert, the drops of blood dripping from it became poisonous serpents and lizards. Before crossing the Sahara on his way from the Atlantic to Ethiopia (the vagueness of the ancients about the location of Ethiopia explains why he went there on his way to Seriphos, Polydectes' island), Perseus paused to use the Gorgon's head to turn Atlas to stone. He is now Mount Atlas.

Rescue of Andromeda and Return of Perseus

Cepheus was actually a kinsman of Perseus, being the brother of his great-great-great-grandfather Danaus. (This confusion of generations is common in mythology.) When Perseus and Andromeda went to Seriphos they left their eldest son, Perses, with Cepheus; Perses became the ancestor of the Persians. Another son, Alcaeus, was the father of Anaxo, the mother of Alcmene, Hercules' mother. Alcmene's father, Electryon, was also a son of Perseus and Andromeda. Hence Hercules was both the great- and the great-great-grandson of Perseus.

In the more common version of the story, Perseus was unwilling to succeed his grandfather, since he had killed him, and traded realms with his cousin Megapenthes, thus becoming King of Tiryns. The Kings of Tiryns thereafter called themselves the Perseids, "Descendants of Perseus."

Upon their deaths, Cepheus, Cassiopeia, Perseus, Andromeda, and the sea-monster (Cetus) were taken to heaven to become constellations.

The representation of Medusa's head as a round grinning face with protruding tongue, which appears often in ancient art, is called a gorgoneion. (See Athena's aegis in the illustrations on pages 148, 160, and 174 in the text.) It is a common apotropaic talisman and was depicted on shields, on city walls and gates and in tombs. It may have served a dual purpose, as representation and as talisman, in the metope shown on p. 145 of the text, since the grin is otherwise obviously inappropriate. Other staring, grinning faces than Medusa's may be used to keep the evil spirits away: for example, the face of Charon in the tomb-painting from Paestum shown on p. 229, which is modeled in the stucco as well as being painted.

Early Adventures of Theseus

Theseus differs from the rest of the great heroes in that he was slight of build and won his victories by intelligence rather than brute force. He was a wrestler and was thought to be the inventor of most of the holds in that sport. He was only sixteen when he made his dangerous journey along the isthmus of Corinth. This journey, during which he cleared the route of monsters and bandits, was the Athenian equivalent of the labors of the Theban/Argive Hercules. The Labors of Theseus were six:

1. The killing of Periphetes of Epidaurus with his own iron club, which Theseus wrested from him and afterwards carried.

2. The killing of Sinis, the "Pine-bender," who would waylay and capture travelers, then tie them to the tops of two pine trees which he had bent down, so that they would be torn in two when he released the trees.

3. The hunting and destruction of Phaea, a monstrous wild sow which devastated the land between Corinth and Megara.

4. Near Megara the bandit Sciron would rob travelers and then, sitting on the edge of the cliffs, compel them to wash his feet. As they were

doing so, he would kick them into the sea, where they were devoured by a giant tortoise. Theseus, however, suspecting Sciron's intentions, seized his feet and threw him over his shoulder into the sea, where he was eaten.

5. Cercyon, the King of Eleusis, a son of Poseidon, wrestled all strangers to the death, but was no match for Theseus' skill.

6. Procrustes, another son of Poseidon, who lived between Eleusis and Athens, was killed as described in the text.

Theseus and the Minotaur

By the time Theseus arrived in Athens, his father had married Medea. Realizing who Theseus was, she prevented Aegeus from seeing him and persuaded him to send the young stranger to kill the huge bull which was ravaging the plain of Marathon. This was the same bull which Minos had failed to sacrifice, which had become the sire of the Minotaur, and which Hercules (Seventh Labor) had brought to Greece. Theseus killed it and returned. Aegeus, who was much under the influence of his enchantress wife, was persuaded by her to allow her to poison this dangerous young man at a banquet celebrating his safe return. Before picking up the wine cup, however, Theseus drew his sword to cut his meat. Aegeus, recognizing the sword, prevented his son from drinking the poison. Foiled, Medea disappeared into the air with Medus, her son by Aegeus.

The confusion of mythological chronology, as well as the desire of every city to insist on the importance of its local hero, is well illustrated by the Athenian claim that Theseus was one of the Argonauts. This is manifestly in conflict with their story that Aegeus met Medea, already living in Corinth, when he was on his way to Troezen to beget Theseus. It is also in conflict with the well-known notion that the Argo was the first ship ever built, since Theseus had already sailed to Crete and back by the time he is supposed to have joined the Argonauts. There is a similar claim that he joined in the Calydonian Boar Hunt.

For the story behind Athens' annual tribute to Crete, and for a further account of the Labyrinth, see the comments on *Europa and her Kin* in Lesson 3.

Later Adventures of Theseus

The sea into which Aegeus threw himself was called the *Aegean* from his name.

By the Amazon Antiope (Shakespeare calls her Hippolyta) Theseus became the father of Hippolytus, who, being devoted to hunting, was a votary of Artemis and hence neglected Aphrodite. To punish him, Aphrodite made his stepmother Phaedra fall in love with him. When he refused her advances she hanged herself, but left for Theseus a letter in which she accused Hippolytus of having attempted her virtue. (Compare the story of Joseph and Potiphar's wife, in the Book of Genesis.) Poseidon had promised Theseus the granting of three wishes; in his rage he now used one of these to wish his son dead. So, as Hippolytus was driving along the seashore, Poseidon sent a monstrous bull from the sea, which frightened the horses so that they overturned the chariot and dragged the young man to death. At the request of Artemis, Asclepius restored Hippolytus to life (for which he himself was killed by the thunderbolt of Zeus). Artemis took Hippolytus with her to Aricia (near modern Nemi) in Italy, where he was worshipped along with her under the name of Virbius.

It was after the death of Phaedra that Theseus abducted Helen, wishing to make her his wife when she came of age, and joined Pirithous in the ill-fated expedition to abduct Persephone. On his return he found not only that Helen was gone, but that his kingdom was in the hands of a usurper. Unable to regain his former influence, he retired to the island of Scyros as the guest of its king, Lycomedes, who treacherously killed him by pushing him off a cliff.

It was Theseus who united the villages of Attica with Athens in a single nation; it was also he who received the exiled Oedipus and gave him a final resting-place.

Bellerophon

Bellerophon (a grandson of Sisyphus) had fled Corinth because of a blood-feud and took refuge at the court of King Proetus of Argos. Proetus was the twin brother of Acrisius and the father of that Megapenthes with whom Perseus later exchanged kingdoms. He had become the King of Tiryns when Acrisius assumed the crown of Argos. Proetus' wife, Anteia, daughter of King Iobates of Lycia, fell in love with Bellerophon, and when he refused her she accused him to her husband of having made advances to her (compare the story of Phaedra and Hippolytus). Not wishing to kill a man who had come to him as a suppliant, Proetus asked Bellerophon to carry a sealed letter to Iobates. In the letter were instructions to Iobates to put Bellerophon to death. This Iobates tried to do by sending him to kill the Chimera, and later by other plots and direct attacks. When Bellerophon survived them all, Iobates was so impressed with the young man's strength and courage that he gave him his own daughter's hand in marriage, and eventually his kingdom.

According to some accounts Bellerophon was not killed by his fall, but lamed and blinded, and spent the rest of his life wandering the earth as an outcast.

Damon and Pythias

This story, so far as we know, is history, not myth or legend but, as the series of events which it describes were repeated in so many later legends, it has legitimately entered the realm of mythology. The story, with different names and setting, was especially popular in the Middle Ages.

PRACTICAL APPLICATIONS

_____ Specific Literary References _____

1. The reference is to Theseus killing the Minotaur.

2. Minerva bore the gorgoneion on her aegis.

3. Pegasus is the winged horse, offspring of Poseidon and Medusa.

4. The Gray Sisters, who shared one eye among them.

5. The tower in which Acrisius imprisoned Danae was made of brass; Zeus came to her disguised as a shower of gold.

6. A reference to the famous friends who were willing to die for each other.

7. The earth is to the stars as Danae was to the shower of gold.

8. Full of windings and confusing passages, like the Cretan Labyrinth.

9. Pallas bore the gorgoneion on her aegis, with which she could cause lightning and thunder.

10. The reference is to the moment when Ariadne awakens to find that Theseus and his fellow Athenians have deserted her on the island of Naxos. This is a popular subject with poets (see, for example, Catullus 64).

_____ Word Study _____

1. The *Chimera* was the most oddly put together of monsters, with a serpent's head on the end of her tail and a goat's head sticking up out

of the middle of her back. The *Labyrinth* was so large and complex that it was impossible to find one's way out of it without help.

3. Jupiter/Zeus, Neptune/Poseidon, Mercury/Hermes, Minerva/Athena.

4. To force something to fit; to embark on a flight of fancy, to draw the long bow, to start on an overly ambitious course; to tilt at windmills, to make a mountain out of a molehill; true to the death (Jonathan's friendship for David continued even when his father Saul was seeking David to kill him).

_____ Questions for Review _____

1. That he would be killed by a child of hers.

2. By imprisoning her in a tower of brass. Zeus entered through the roof, disguised as a shower of gold, and begot Perseus.

3. By enclosing him and his mother in a chest and casting it into the sea. The chest drifted to the island of Seriphos, where mother and child were rescued by a fisherman.

4. He felt that he was in the way of his wooing of Danae.

5. To bring back the head of Medusa.

6. A monster with claws of brass and snakes for hair, the sight of whose face turned people to stone.

7. Minerva's and Mercury's.

8. By using a polished shield as a mirror so that he did not have to look at her face, and by using a sickle or scimitar instead of a sword so that he could catch her neck in the curve of it without having to aim a blow.

9. Andromeda.

10. To petrify Phineus and his followers, and Polydectes and his army.

11. He gave it to Minerva.

12. He left Argos.

13. By being accidentally struck by a discus which slipped from Perseus' hand.

14. King Aegeus of Athens.

15. To send him to Athens as soon as he was strong enough to lift the rock under which Aegeus had hidden his sword and sandals.

16. When, at sixteen, he was able to lift the rock.

17. He killed Periphetes [Sinis, Phaea, Sciron, Cercyon] and Procrustes.

18. The killing of the Minotaur.

19. The son of Pasiphae and Poseidon's bull, a monster half man and half bull.

20. Ariadne's; she gave him a sword and the famous Clue of Ariadne to enable him to find his way out of the Labyrinth. If he was, he didn't show it: he abandoned her on Naxos while she was sleeping.

21. Theseus forgot to change his sails from black to white, a signal that he was still alive.

22. A fire-breathing monster which, reading from front to back, was a lion, a goat, and a serpent.

23. By borrowing Pegasus, the winged horse which belonged to the Muses.

24. By attempting to fly up to heaven, whereupon Zeus sent a gadfly to sting Pegasus, which caused Bellerophon to fall.

25. Damon and Pythias.

26. Damon was willing to die in his friend's place; Pythias was willing to return and die to save his friend from dying.

_____ Reading List _____

Mary Renault's *The King Must Die* and *The Bull from the Sea* are extremely clever and able euhemerizations of the myth of Theseus. She manages to rationalize every single incident of his career. The books tell an absorbing story, but — more than that — they depict very accurately what modern studies suggest the situation must have been when the worship of the Goddess was giving way to the worship of the Olympians. Hence they are a painless way of absorbing a good deal of information about the early history of western religion. They also provide a convincing example of how historical facts might have become myth. Whether or not you can recommend them will depend upon your school's policy and the age of your students, since they contain some scenes of sexual activity.

11   Adventures of Hercules

Birth and Early Life

Jupiter became the father of Hercules in the same way that Uther Pendragon became the father of Arthur, by assuming the form of his mother's husband. He did this while Amphitryon was away at war, pretending that he had sneaked back secretly to see his wife. The natural confusion resulting when the real Amphitryon returned and heard that he had already paid a night visit has comic or even farcical aspects, and in fact has been a favorite subject of comic playwrights from antiquity to the present. Since Amphitryon begot Iphicles in the same night as Hercules was begotten by Zeus, the two were twins, though only half-brothers.

At least five different cities claimed Hercules as a national hero, and still others had their own myths about him; hence his mythology has many variant forms. The difficulty is compounded by the fact that no ancient connected account of Hercules' life has come down to us, though he appears peripherally in many stories and there are very many passing references to him.

His parents belonged to the royal house of Tiryns or Argos, both being Perseids. Amphitryon was the son of Alcaeus the son of Perseus and Andromeda; while Alcmene's father was Electryon, Alcaeus' brother, and her mother was Anaxo, Alcaeus' daughter and Amphitryon's sister. In other words, both Electryon and Amphitryon were married to their own nieces. The Theban connection is through Amphitryon's mother (Alcmene's grandmother), Alcaeus' wife Hipponome, who was a sister of Jocasta, the mother (and later the wife) of Oedipus, and of Jocasta's brother Creon, who was King of Thebes in Hercules' day and the father of Hercules' wife Megara. Amphitryon and his wife were forced to leave the Peloponnesus for Thebes because Amphitryon had inadvertently slain his father-in-law/brother-in-law Electryon. Therefore, Hercules was born at Thebes.

On the day Hercules was to be born, Jupiter announced to the other gods that on that day a descendant of Perseus who would rule over all the Perseids was about to be born. When Juno heard this irrevocable statement, she hurried to Argos (or Mycenae or Tiryns) and hastened the labor of Nicippe, wife of Sthenelus, son of Perseus (and brother of Alcaeus and Electryon). At the same time she sent her servant, the goddess of childbirth, to Thebes to prevent the birth of Hercules. This she did by sitting on the doorstep of Amphitryon's palace and tying knots in a cord. Once Juno informed her that Eurystheus son of Sthenelus had been born she undid the knots, and Alcmene gave birth to Hercules after seven days of labor. After another day of labor she bore Iphicles.

In some accounts another of Hercules' tutors was Chiron the Centaur, who taught him the sciences.

Marriage and Madness

As time went on, the original Hercules of the myths began to be depicted in two quite different ways. In one he is physically huge and muscular (like the "Farnese Hercules" in the National Museum at Naples), very fond of eating, drinking, and making love, obliging but not overly sensitive, quick-tempered but slow-witted, much more brawn than brain. He is sometimes almost a comic figure, as in his famous drunk scene in the *Alcestis* of Euripides, or when he lets Atlas trick him into holding up the sky.

In the other he is an intelligent, compassionate savior-god, who performs his task of ridding the world of its plagues and monsters from a desire to aid humanity rather than to display his prowess. Depictions in the plastic arts show him as a well-built but by no means muscle-bound youth. This Hercules is the one who became the patron god and symbol of the Cynic and Stoic philosophers who were the inventors of the myth of the Choice of Hercules. More than that, he became during the period of the conflict of religions (the Ⅲd Century of our era) a kind of Messiah figure. He was addressed as "Savior" in prayers, and his Labors were reinterpreted in a symbolic way to show him as the savior of humanity. The final three labors, for example, all represented his victory over Death. The last stand of paganism against the rise of Christianity set up Jupiter and Hercules as its own God the Father and God the Son in rivalry with those of the Christians. A third pair of gods, the Unconquered Sun and his son Mithras, joined in the fray. The Ⅲd Century saw a strange conflict among these three divine dyads, a conflict which apparently seemed quite real to their worshippers, until the Christian pair, championed by Constantine, was victorious at the Battle of the Milvian Bridge. This set Constantine firmly on the throne and marked the beginning of the downfall of paganism.

There may for a time have been a fourth savior-god. The good Emperor Alexander Severus (A.D. 222-235) is said to have had statues of Hercules, Mithras, Jesus, and Moses in his private chapel.

Megara was the daughter of Creon, the brother of Jocasta and King of Thebes after Oedipus had gone into exile and his two sons had been killed in their struggle for the throne.

The First Six Labors

In some versions of the myth, Hercules, whose name had hitherto been Alcaeus or Alcides, was told by the Oracle at Delphi to change his name to Heracles ("Glory of Hera") as a token of his future reconciliation with the goddess, and to undergo the penance of service to her through his labors performed for her favorite, Eurystheus.

Labor I. The Nemean Lion, the offspring of the Chimera and Orthus, was invulnerable. Its skin could be penetrated only by its own claws.

Labor II. The Hydra was another child of Typhon and Echidna. Eurystheus refused to count this adventure as one of the Labors, on the grounds that Hercules had had help.

Labor III. Hercules pursued the Arcadian stag all the way to the source of the Danube and back again. The source of the Danube was thought to be in the Rhipaean Mountains, the starting-point of the north wind, beyond which lived the Hyperboreans.

Labor IV. When Hercules returned with the Erymanthian Boar, Eurystheus was so frightened by the sight of it that he crawled into an underground storage jar. He ordered Hercules thereafter to make his deliveries outside the city walls from which he could inspect them in safety.

Some of Hercules' Labors included what the Greeks called *parerga*, "side-tasks." For example, on his way to kill the Erymanthian Boar Hercules stopped to visit his friend, the Centaur Pholus, who lived in Arcadia. Pholus had a jar of wine, a gift from Bacchus himself, which Hercules insisted on opening, despite his host's warnings. Attracted by the smell of the wine, the other Centaurs gathered and soon a fight broke out in which Hercules accidentally shot his old tutor, Chiron, with one of his poisoned arrows. Being the only immortal Centaur, Chiron could not die, but suffered great agony. Pholus himself died after pulling a poisoned arrow from one of his dead friends and grazing his foot with it.

Labor V. Another *parergon* occurred after the Fifth Labor. Augeas had agreed to pay Hercules for this labor with one-tenth of his cattle but, when he found out that Hercules had to do the task anyway, refused payment. Hercules later returned and killed Augeas and all his sons, and then founded the Olympic Games in honor of the deed.

Labor VI. The Stymphalides had been raised by Mars. Some of them escaped Hercules' arrows and settled on the island of Aretias in the Black Sea, where the Argonauts met and fought with them.

The Last Six Labors

Labor VII. The Cretan Bull was the same bull which Neptune had sent from the sea in answer to Minos' prayer for a worthy sacrifice. As a punishment to Minos for keeping it for himself, the bull became the father, by Minos' wife Pasiphae, of the Minotaur, then went mad and ravaged the island. Released by Hercules after having been shown to Eurystheus, the bull wandered from the Peloponnesus to Marathon in Attica where it was captured and sacrificed by Theseus, but to Apollo, not Neptune.

Labor VIII. Diomedes was a son of Mars and King of the Bistones in Thrace. Hercules began by stealing the horses with the help of his friend Abderus. When Diomedes and his army pursued them to the coast, Hercules left Abderus in charge of the mares while he defeated the army. Returning to find that Abderus had been eaten, Hercules fed Diomedes to the mares in revenge, and founded the town of Abdera in memory of his friend. (In historical times this town had a reputation for stupidity. It was an insult to call someone an "Abderite.") Even though the mares were now tame, Eurystheus was afraid to keep them. He released them and they eventually wandered to Mt. Olympus, where they were eaten by wild beasts.

Labor IX. Hippolyte was the sister of Antiope, Theseus' wife. One of Hercules' most famous *parerga* was performed during this Labor. Neptune and Apollo, having displeased Jupiter, had been sentenced to serve King Laomedon of Troy for wages. Together with Aeacus, son of Zeus and Aegina, they built the walls of Troy but, upon completion of the work, Laomedon refused to pay them their promised wages. Neptune punished him by sending a sea-monster to ravage his land until he agreed to let his daughter Hesione be devoured by it. Hercules, returning from the city of the Amazons, saw Hesione chained to a rock, made inquiries and then offered to kill the monster if Laomedon would give him the marvelous horses which his grandfather Tros had received from Jupiter in exchange for Ganymede (Tros' son). Laomedon agreed but, when Hercules killed the monster, he refused to give him the horses. Therefore Hercules declared war on Laomedon.

Labor X. Geryon (who is usually said to have had three bodies) was a son of Chrysaor, who was a brother of Pegasus, both children of Neptune and Medusa. Eurytion's two-headed dog Orthus was actually Geryon's nephew, being (like Cerberus) a child of his sister Echidna.

The boat in which Hercules reached the island was the golden bowl in which the Sun made his nightly return journey from west to east. Most accounts make Hercules return from Erythea by the overland route, driving the cattle through Spain and along the coast as far as (for some unknown reason) Sicily, then north along the east coast of Italy and so to Greece. Many *parerga* are assigned to this journey.

At the mouth of the Rhone he was prevented from crossing by the Ligyes who showered arrows upon him from the other bank. He had spent all his own arrows and was on the point of being overwhelmed. Suddenly Jupiter sent from the sky a shower of stones which Hercules used as missiles to defeat the Ligyes. In historical times the area was a plain littered with large rocks; this may have given rise to the story.

Hercules paused to rest near the future site of Rome. While he was sleeping, a gigantic fire-breathing son of Vulcan, Cacus, stole some of the cattle and dragged them into his cave by their tails so that their footprints appeared to lead from, not toward, the cave. Hercules was fooled by this trick but, when he began to drive the rest of the herd away, the cattle missed their companions and lowed, and the imprisoned cattle answered. After a fierce fight, Hercules killed Cacus.

In Sicily one of the cattle strayed away. When Hercules went to look for it he found it in the possession of Eryx, a son of Neptune (or of Butes, a descendant of Neptune) and Venus. Though Eryx was a great boxer and in fact the inventor of the sport, Hercules defeated and killed him.

As Hercules rounded the north shore of the Adriatic, Juno, seeing that he was nearing his goal, sent a gadfly which scattered the herd across Thessaly and throughout Thrace. He was then forced to go as far as the Hellespont to round them up.

While crossing the Isthmus of Pallene in Macedonia, Hercules was attacked by Alcyoneus, the oldest and most powerful of the Giants, who threw a huge rock at him. Using his club, Hercules batted the rock back at him. It would have killed him, but Alcyoneus could not be killed while he was on his home ground of Pallene. He was, however, stunned, so that Hercules was able to escape with the herd. The rock, large enough to cover twelve wagons, was shown to tourists in antiquity.

Upon the return of Hercules, Eurytheus sacrificed the cattle to Juno.

Labor XI. Hercules' route, on his way to find the Apples of the Hesperides, is even more illogical than that of his return from Erythea. These strange roundabout journeys are caused partly by an attempt to include local hero legends in the Hercules story, partly by vague geographical knowledge, and partly by disagreements of various authors about the location of certain events. The garden where the Hesperides dwelt was the garden of the gods themselves, the scene of the wedding of Jupiter and Juno. The golden apples were a wedding present from Gaea to Juno, who left them in the garden with the Hesperides and the hundred-headed serpent Ladon (son of Phorcys and Ceto) to guard them. This garden, and Atlas, were located by some authors in the land of the Hyperboreans at the back of the North Wind, and by others in the far west on the shores of Ocean. The latter view eventually prevailed and the modern Mt. Atlas marks the site.

In any case, Hercules began his search by going north to the River Eridanus, the mythical river by which Phaethon fell and where his sisters, metamorphosed into trees, produced amber. Amber did come from the north, from the Baltic, in fact; but later writers identify the Eridanus with the Po in Italy. Hercules asked the nymphs of the river for help and they referred him to Nereus, the omniscient sea-god, whom Hercules eventually found on the north shore of Africa. Having kept his grasp on him through all of his changes of shape (Nereus shared this habit with Proteus), Hercules received the answer that the gods were pledged not to reveal the location and that he must go and ask Prometheus, the rebel god. This story is probably meant to explain Hercules' travels thereafter. Originally he may have gone north because Nereus had told him that the garden lay in the land of the Hyperboreans.

Hercules, on his way to the Caucasus, where Prometheus lay bound, now traveled westward along the African coast to Libya where he met and wrestled Antaeus, son of Neptune and Gaea. When he reached Egypt he found that its king was Busiris, a son of a daughter of Epaphus by Neptune. Under Busiris' rule Egypt had suffered nine years of bad harvests because of the Nile's failure to rise sufficiently (as in the case of the seven lean years in the story of Joseph). Busiris had sent for Phrasius, a prophet from Cyprus, who had advised him to sacrifice to Jupiter all strangers who entered Egypt. This Busiris did, beginning with Phrasius himself. When Hercules arrived he allowed himself to be bound and brought to the altar. Then, bursting his bonds, he killed Busiris and his sons and followers.

Arriving next in Ethiopia, Hercules found his progress opposed by King Emathion, a son of Aurora and Tithonus, who had usurped the throne from his brother Memnon. Hercules killed him and restored Memnon.

One of the conditions set by Jupiter for the freeing of Prometheus (which was the next of the *parerga* of the Eleventh Labor) was that another immortal must volunteer to die for him. It was satisfied by Chiron, still constantly in agony from the Hydra's poison on the arrow with which Hercules had accidentally shot him. Set free, Prometheus in gratitude gladly told Hercules that the secret of the location of the garden was known only to Atlas, the grandfather of the Hesperides.

Having left Prometheus' crag in the Caucasus, Hercules followed the shore of Ocean around the disk of the world, passing through the land of the Hyperboreans, until he arrived at Atlas. Atlas refused to tell Hercules where the garden was. This was his excuse for going himself to get the apples and persuading Hercules to hold up the sky.

When Eurystheus received the apples he was afraid to keep them himself, so Hercules dedicated them to Athena, who returned them to the garden.

Labor XII. So dreadful was the appearance of Cerberus that when he was brought into the light the sun, which had just risen, turned back and went down again, setting in the east. Eurystheus refused to emerge from his storage jar to look at him. The *parerga* of this labor were the freeing of Theseus and a son of Acheron, Ascalaphus, who had been the only one to see Proserpina eat the pomegranate seeds and who had informed on her to Pluto. For this reason Proserpina was now keeping Ascalaphus prisoner, though Pluto, who was grateful to him, was glad to have the excuse to let him go. Proserpina still had her revenge, however. As Ascalaphus left the Lower World she turned him into an owl.

Later Career

In gratitude for his help with Hydra, Hercules gave Iolaus his wife Megara, and went to woo Iole, the daughter of King Eurytus of Oechalia, his former tutor in archery. Iole had been promised to anyone who could defeat her father in a contest with the bow. Hercules won, but Eurytus and all his family except his son Iphitus refused him his reward on the grounds that he had killed his own children.

At about this time the cattle-thief Autolycus stole Eurytus' cattle and Eurytus accused Hercules of the deed. In search of the cattle, Hercules came to the palace of Admetus where he rescued Alcestis from Death or Hades. He was joined by his friend Iphitus, whom he received hospitably but then killed in another fit of madness sent by Juno. Having recovered his sanity, he asked King Neleus of Pylus (a son of Neptune) to purify him, but Neleus refused and Hercules fell ill as a result of his crime.

He next went to Delphi to beg Apollo to heal him but Apollo refused, whereupon Hercules seized the sacred tripod on which the Pythia sat to deliver her oracles, and would have carried it away if Apollo had not intercepted him. They fought and in the end Jupiter had to part his two sons with his lightning; Apollo then told Hercules that he could be cured only by hiring himself out for three years and paying his earnings to Eurytus. Mercury arranged for his service to Queen Omphale.

After his period of employment was over, Hercules joined the Argonauts but never completed the expedition, having been left behind in Mysia while he searched for Hylas. But when the Argonauts returned he enlisted the boldest of them (including Peleus and Telamon, the sons of Aeacus and the fathers, respectively, of Achilles and Ajax) for the war which he had declared against Laomedon of Troy. The heroes sailed in eighteen ships to this war, the First Trojan War, in which Hercules killed with his poisoned arrows Laomedon and all his sons except Tithonus, who had already left to go to Aurora, and one baby boy for whose life his sister Hesione pleaded. The baby was thereafter called Priam ("Ransom"); he grew up to be Troy's king and lose the Second Trojan War. Hesione was given to Telamon. Priam later sent his brother-in-law Antenor to bring her back to Troy. The Greeks' refusal to release her was one of the first causes of the Second Trojan War.

At about this time, the Giants, borne (some say) by Gaea to get revenge on the Olympians for their overthrow of the Titans, attempted to storm Mt. Olympus by piling Mt. Pelion on Mt. Ossa. In this they failed, but a great battle took place between the gods and the Giants on the volcanic Macedonian peninsula of Pallene. The Giants were led by Hercules' old enemy Alcyoneus. The Olympians knew from a prophecy that they could not win without the help of a mortal. Their natural choice was Hercules, whom Athena summoned to the battle. He dragged Alcyoneus, who could not be killed on his own ground, away from Pallene and then shot him with a poisoned arrow. Then, in the same way, he killed each of the Giants as they were thrown to the earth by the gods. The Giant Enceladus, seeing the carnage, ran away, but Athena threw a large rock at him which sank him in the sea. The rock was the island of Sicily. (The story is obviously in conflict with the story that Hercules had already visited Sicily in his Tenth Labor.) Other Giants fled to the island of Cos, but Neptune broke off the piece where they were and hurled it upside down into the sea where it became the island of Nisyrus.

Hercules now went to Pylus where, in revenge for Neleus' refusal to purify him after the murder of Iphitus, he killed all his sons except Nestor, who was away from home at the time, and Periclymenus, who escaped after a fierce resistance. He even wounded Pluto himself who had come from the Lower World to assist the Pylians. In another war, this time against the Lacedaemonians, his ally was King Cepheus of Tegea, by whose sister Auge he became the father of Telephus, the Greeks' guide on their way to Troy in the Trojan War.

Hercules answered Meleager's call to join the Calydonian Boar Hunt and remained afterwards to marry Deianira. He and his new wife stayed with his father-in-law for three years. When Hercules accidentally killed a boy at a banquet, he was required by law to go into exile. On his way to Trachis to stay with his nephew Ceyx, he killed Nessus.

While staying with Ceyx, Hercules was given another task, this time by Apollo. Apollo wanted him to kill the robber Cycnus, a son of Mars, who was waylaying the processions on their way to Delphi. In the combat Mars aided his son, while Hercules was supported by Athena and his nephew Iolaus. Hercules not only killed Cycnus (who became a swan), but even wounded Mars himself.

Hercules next determined to get his revenge on Eurytus for refusing him his daughter Iole. He took Oechalia, killed Eurytus and all his sons, and captured Iole. Wishing to make a thanksgiving sacrifice to his father Jupiter, Hercules sent for the fatal robe, because it was necessary to be clothed in white for the ceremony. The blood of the Hydra, which had entered Nessus' bloodstream from Hercules' arrow, was such a powerful poison that when Hercules attempted to tear the robe off, it tore pieces of his flesh away. On his funeral pyre he gave Iole to his son (by Deianira) Hyllus, and his bow and arrows to Poeas, King of the Malians, who lived at the foot of Mt. Oeta, on which the pyre was laid. Deianira, realizing what she had done, hanged herself.

Received among the gods, Hercules was married to Hebe. He was one of a very small number of heroes who became gods and, like the others (e.g. Dionysus and Asclepius), he was very popular: a god who was once human can understand human concerns better than the more remote Olympians. He was of course the patron god of athletes, of gymnasia and baths, and, as the legendary founder of the Olympic Games, also of the Olympic Truce, which stopped all wars and conflicts every four years for the duration of the games. He was worshipped by both Greeks and Romans as the Conqueror, the Invincible, the Guardian, the Defender, the Averter of Evils, the Savior. People about to start on journeys prayed to Hercules the Guide.

In Rome his worship was early, founded (it was thought) by Hercules himself after the killing of Cacus. He was supposed to have built the great altar in the Cattle Market near the Tiber. There he was, oddly enough, associated with the Muses, as Apollo was in Greece. He was considered to be the ancestor of the Latins and of the Roman family of the Fabii. He was also the patron of the Juventus, the association of upper-class boys. This was perhaps through his marriage with Hebe (Juventas).

Hercules was identified with many foreign gods, notably with the Phoenician/Carthaginian Melkart and with one of the Twelve Gods of Egypt.

The complex ramifications of his story and its chronological inconsistencies arise no doubt from the fact that, as his fame grew, his name was given to many local heroes, whose deeds were then included in his legend. Some of his deeds, such as his various wars, may be based on historical events. The ancients were themselves puzzled by these inconsistencies. Some even came to the no doubt correct conclusion that there had been several Herculeses. Herodotus (II, 42-46) is interesting on this subject.

PRACTICAL APPLICATIONS

_____ Specific Literary References _____

1. Unsurpassable, nearly superhuman, after Hercules the Invincible.

2. The Amazons were of course pictured as tall and athletic.

3. A reference to the fact that Antaeus, a son of Gaea, derived strength from contact with his mother the Earth.

4. A reference to the notion that the Hydra grew two new heads for each one lopped off.

5. Alcides is another (or the original) name of Hercules. In this reference, in agony from the Shirt of Nessus, he is building his funeral pyre.

6. In some accounts there are three Hesperides (in others they are four or seven) and they are the daughters of Hesper or Hesperus, rather than of Atlas' daughter Hesperis. The golden tree is the tree on which the apples were hung.

7. The name *Hesperides* is sometimes given to the garden itself and it is occasionally identified with the Fortunate Isles, the Islands of the Blest.

8. "Nerve" in Tudor times meant "sinew." The reference is to the Lion's invulnerability.

_____ Word Study _____

1. *Herculean*: after Hercules, the strongest of all the heroes. *Amazonian*: after the Amazons, a tribe in which the fighting was all done by the women, men being used only for mating and then killed. *Hesperian*: from Hesper (Hesperus), the Evening Star, because at evening the sun sets in the west. *Atlas*: from Atlas; (1) because the heavens were often depicted as a globe which he supports on his neck and shoulders; (2) because Mercator gave the name to his book of maps which had a picture of Atlas on the cover; and (3) because the nearly globular shape of the head suggested the globe which Atlas supports.

2. Calpe and Abyla were thought to be two pillars which Hercules had erected to commemorate his passing the straits. In Algeria or Morocco.

3. The first two refer to the fact that the Labors of Hercules were considered impossible for ordinary mortals. The stable of Augeas contained thirty years' worth of dung from three thousand oxen. The choice between pleasure and duty. To be refreshed by a return to one's origins as Antaeus was by contact with his mother Gaea. Someone or something effective from its very birth, from Hercules' strangling of the serpents in his cradle. Evils which multiply when one tries to eliminate them, as the Hydra's heads grew back twofold.

4. The Amazon.

_____ Questions for Review_____

1. Juno.

2. By sending two serpents to destroy him in his cradle.

3. Choose one: (a) Alcides, which means "valiant," was Hercules' nickname; (b) it was his real original name, later changed to Heracles at the command of Delphi; (c) it is a patronymic, meaning "descendant of Alcaeus" (his paternal grandfather who was also his maternal great-grandfather).

4. Amphitryon, Autolycus, Eurytus, Castor, Linus, Rhadamanthus, and Chiron. (It is a melancholy fact, and a warning to teachers, that he afterwards killed three out of the seven.)

5. A tendency to go mad and kill his loved ones.

6. Of the Thespian.

7. Between Pleasure and Duty; he chose the latter.

8. Megara.

9. Because he had killed his children and two nephews. To enslave himself to his kinsman Eurystheus.

10. Twelve. _i._ The Nemean Lion; he had to kill this invulnerable beast. _ii._ The Lernaean Hydra; he was to kill this nine-headed serpent, each of whose heads was replaced by two as it was cut off. _iii._ The Arcadian (Ceryneian, Maenalian) Stag; this had to be captured alive in spite of its incredible swiftness. _iv._ The Erymanthian Boar; this fierce animal also had to be captured alive. _v._ The Augean Stables; Hercules was required to clean out the stables of a herd of three thousand oxen which had not been cleaned for thirty years. _vi._ The Stymphalian Birds; he was required to kill these man-eating creatures who were able to shoot their bronze feathers like arrows. _vii._ The Cretan Bull; he was expected to capture alive this supernatural, mad creature. _viii._ The Mares of Diomedes; he was to bring home these man-eating mares. _ix._ The Girdle of Hippolyte; Hercules was to bring the belt of the Queen of the Amazons to Admeta. _x._ The Oxen of Geryon; he had to drive home this herd which was guarded by a giant and a monstrous dog. _xi._ The Apples of the Hesperides; this task involved locating the garden where the apples were kept. _xii._ Cerberus; without using any weapons, he was to bring the dreaded monster from the Lower World.

11. When, after his wooing of Iole, he was entertaining her brother Iphitus, whom he killed.

12. To work for wages for three years and to give his pay to Eurytus.

13. Prometheus.

14. A son of Neptune and Gaea; he became stronger every time he touched the earth.

15. By holding him off the ground and strangling him.

16. A daughter of Oeneus and sister of Meleager; she became Hercules' second wife.

17. By donning the Shirt of Nessus, a garment which had been dipped in the blood of the Centaur who had died from an arrow poisoned with the Hydra's blood.

12   Jason and the Golden Fleece

Capturing His Kingdom

The story of Jason and the Argonauts contains many more elements of the folk tale than most myths. It is early (Homer knew of the Argonauts) and may represent some actual early expedition which grew to the proportions of heroic adventure by various processes. In the first place, each important family of Thessaly would insist that one of its ancestors had taken part; as the story grew in importance other communities would add their own heroes to the list. Then finally, as the account grew to be a better and better story, it would attract to itself favorite themes from folklore. Some of these are: (1) the simple test offered by a supernatural being, which the hero passes while the villain fails (in this case, carrying an old woman across a river); (2) the assigning of an impossible task to an unwelcome visitor; (3) the quest in which the hero is aided by friends with different magical talents; and (4) the alliance with the hero of the evil magician's daughter. All these may be found in the tales collected by the brothers Grimm as well as in the folk tales of many lands. Individually the themes are seen in other myths (the second, for example, in the stories of Perseus and Bellerophon; the fourth in the story of Theseus) but nowhere else in the mythology are they so numerous.

Another unusual feature of the myth is that Hera, who is usually the enemy of the hero (Hercules, Aeneas), is here the goddess who helps him, a role usually assigned to Athena. In the usual accounts, Pelias has offended Hera, in later versions by failing to sacrifice to her, but earlier (as happens in folk tales) by a lack of kindness. As he was about to ford a river, she, in the guise of an old woman, asked him to carry her across. He churlishly refused. When she presented herself to Jason with the same request, he willingly carried her, this being the reason why he could not stop to pick up his sandal when it fell off.

The commissioning of Jason with his quest has its homelier folklore version as well. Pelias craftily asked him what he would do if he were king and had learned that a subject wished to harm him. Jason replied that he would order him to fetch the Golden Fleece. This select-your-own-punishment trick is a familiar theme of folk tales, though it is more often used on villains than on heroes. In this case the trick rebounded onto Pelias, for it was Hera who, wishing to bring glory to Jason, had put this answer into his head.

Euhemerists of the Jason-myth have ingeniously suggested that the story is based upon a piratical expedition against some gold-panning community, since one method of recovering gold from a stream was to spread a fleece weighted down with stones on its bed to catch the particles as they drifted downstream. The Phasis in Colchis was, like the Pactolus in Lydia, a gold-bearing stream.

In the myth the story of the fleece itself is connected with the ill-fated House of Cadmus. King Athamas of Orchomenus was in love with Cadmus' daughter Ino, but was required by Hera to marry a cloud-goddess, Nephele, by whom he had two children, Phrixus and Helle. But Athamas continued to love Ino, and eventually Nephele left him. He married Ino and they had two children, Learchus and Melicertes. Jealous of her stepchildren, Ino conceived a plot against them. One year she secretly roasted the grain which was being kept for the next year's planting. When it didn't germinate, ambassadors were sent to Delphi and on their return Ino bribed them to say that the god had demanded the sacrifice of Phrixus to Zeus. Nephele saved her children with the help of Hermes' golden ram. Ino was punished by Hera both for her cruelty and for having nursed the infant Dionysus: Athamas went mad and drove her and Melicertes into the sea.

In Colchis Aeetes gave Phrixus Medea's sister Chalciope for his wife. Phrixus sent his two sons back to Orchomenus; one of them was Argus, an Argonaut and the builder of the *Argo*.

Voyage of the Argo

The *Argo*, designed by Athena, is said by many authors to have been the first ship ever built. The oak of the figurehead was from the grove of Zeus at Dodona where the oracle of the god was conveyed by the rustling of the leaves of the oak trees.

The fifty heroes who accompanied Jason fall into three categories. The earliest list consists only of heroes of the Minyans, a prehistoric tribe of Iolcus and Orchomenus: Acastus (Pelias' son and a good friend of Jason), Admetus, Argus, Erginus (a son of Poseidon and King of Orchomenus after the exile of Athamas), Euphemus (a son of Poseidon and married to Hercules' sister Laonome), Periclymenus (a son of Neleus who was later to fight Hercules at Pylus), and Tiphys (the steersman of the *Argo*). To this list were then added all the heroes of the various nations who belonged to the generation before the Trojan War, or were the fathers of Trojan War heroes, or were the ancestors of families prominent in historical times: Atalanta, Castor and Pollux, Meleager, Nestor, Hercules, Theseus, Butes (ancestor of a noble family of Athens), Peleus (father of Achilles), Telamon (father of Ajax), and Tydeus (father of Diomedes). Finally there were what students of folklore call the Talented Companions, the hero's assistants (familiar from fairy tales) who have specialized magical abilities: Amphiaraus, Idmon, and Mopsus (who could all foretell the future), Ancaeus and Idas (along with Hercules the three strongest men in the world), Idas' brother Lynceus (who was so far- and sharp-sighted that he could see into the heart of the earth), Orpheus (who could move even inanimate objects by his music), and Zetes and Calais (who could fly). Two of the original list who were not otherwise famous were also assigned magical talents: Euphemus could run over the top of the sea without wetting his feet and Periclymenus could, like Proteus, change himself into any shape.

The women of Lemnos had neglected to sacrifice to Aphrodite. As a punishment she made them smell so bad that their husbands imported other women from Thrace. Enraged by this infidelity the Lemnian women plotted and executed a massacre of all the men on the island. By the time of the Argonauts' visit they had perhaps lost their smell; at any rate the Argonauts (except for Hercules and Hylas) mated with them, and Hypsipyle, their queen, bore twin sons to Jason.

Having passed through the Hellespont, the Argonauts stopped at Cyzicus in the land of the Doliones. They were received hospitably by King Cyzicus (for whom the city was named); but when they left they were driven back by a storm at night and were mistaken by the Doliones for pirates. In a skirmish in the dark the Argonauts mistakenly killed Cyzicus.

It was at Cios on the coast of Mysia that Hercules was left behind; the boxer Amycus was King of the Bebryces, in Bithynia; Phineus lived at Salmydessus in Thrace. Phineus had been married to Cleopatra, a daughter of Boreas and sister of Calais and Zetes, and had had two sons by her. However, he tired of her, imprisoned her, and married Idaea, a daughter of Dardanus. Idaea hated her stepsons and slandered them to Phineus. Believing her, Phineas punished them by putting out their eyes and imprisoning them with their mother. For this deed he was punished by Zeus who gave him a choice of penalties, death or blindness, never again to see the sun. He chose never to see the sun. The choice so enraged Helios that he sent the Harpies to plague him.

The islands where the sons of Boreas turned back from their pursuit were from that time on called the Strophades, the Islands of Turning. Hera sent Iris to make the Harpies swear that they would never leave these islands. Returning to Salmydessus, Zethes and Calais sent Idaea back to her father and released their sister and her sons from the dungeon. The sons, whose eyesight Hera restored, were placed on their father's throne.

Having passed through the Symplegades into the Black Sea, the Argonauts stopped in the land of the Mariandynians in Bithynia where they were hospitably received by Lycus, its king. Here Apollo's son, Idmon the seer, was killed by a boar during a hunt. His prophetic powers had told him that he would die on the expedition, but he had preferred a short and glorious life to a long and ignoble one. At Apollo's orders the city later to be called Heraclea-in-Pontus was built around his tomb. Tiphys, too, died here of a disease, and was revered thereafter as a kind of patron saint of steersmen. His place was taken by Ancaeus.

Passing by the land of the Amazons, the *Argo* came to the island of Aretias where her crew were threatened by the Stymphalian birds that had escaped from Hercules and taken refuge here. The Argonauts drove them away and rescued Cytissorus, son of Phrixus and brother of Argus, who had been shipwrecked on the island on his way to Orchomenus.

Winning the Golden Fleece

Medea demonstrated both her cleverness and her ruthlessness in delaying her father's pursuit of the *Argo*. She killed her young brother Absyrtus, whom she had brought with her in her flight, and having cut up his body, dropped the pieces overboard as they sailed, knowing that Aeetes must pause to retrieve and reassemble the body of his son for a funeral.

There are numerous routes assigned to the *Argo's* homeward voyage by different traditions. Brief descriptions of some of them may provide an illustration of ancient ideas of geography. In some accounts she sailed, not out into the Black Sea, but up Colchis' river, the Phasis, to where it flowed from the River Ocean. She then followed the Ocean around the east and south coasts of Asia and Africa. The Argonauts landed in Africa and, after a twelve-day portage, brought their ship to Lake Tritonis (the great salt lake, *Sebkha Farun*, south of Tunis, imagined in antiquity to be much larger than it really was).

In other accounts the Argonauts crossed the Black Sea and sailed up the Danube to the point where the Rhine branched from it (!), then down the Rhine to the North Sea, then south along the Ocean to the Pillars of Hercules and into the Mediterranean that way. As they drew near to the Peloponnesus they were driven back by a storm onto the great sandbar, the Syrtes, off the coast of Libya. With the help of Hera and Poseidon they dislodged the *Argo* from the sands and made their way by a channel into Lake Tritonis.

Another version sent them up the Danube to where the Po branched from it (!), then down the Po to the Adriatic. They intended to put in at Corcyra, but were driven back by a storm in which the ship was almost lost. The figurehead (the speaking oak from Dodona) warned them that they could not land in any Greek land until Medea had been purified from the murder of Absyrtus by her aunt Circe, Aeetes' sister, a powerful sorceress who lived on the island of Aeaea off the west coast of Italy. They accordingly sailed back up the Po to where it branched from the Rhone (!), then down the Rhone to the Tyrrhenian Sea and Aeaea.

All these imaginary interconnections of the rivers of Europe with each other undoubtedly reflect wishful thinking on the part of the Greeks, who very much disliked the open sea and seldom sailed out of the sight of land. In much the same way, European settlers in North America clung as long as they could to their belief in a "Northwest Passage," a route from the Atlantic up the St. Lawrence, across the Great Lakes, and down an unfortunately imaginary river which was supposed to flow from Lake Superior to the Pacific.

From Aeaea, according to this last version, they sailed past the island of the Sirens, from whom they were saved by the song of Orpheus, which turned the Sirens to stone. Unfortunately, before Orpheus could begin his song, Butes was so charmed by the Sirens that he leaped overboard and would have drowned if Aphrodite had not saved him and brought him to Sicily where he became by her the father of Eryx. This conflicts chronologically with the story that Hercules had by this time already met and killed Eryx (Labor X). Another indication that Hercules was not originally one of the Argonauts is the story that as they neared Colchis the Argonauts glimpsed Prometheus on his crag and felt the wind of the fanning of the wings of his vulture.

The next dangers to threaten the Argonauts were Scylla and Charybdis, but Hera sent sea nymphs to their aid, who guided the *Argo* through the exact middle of the channel just out of reach of both monsters.

Arriving at the land of the Phaeacians, they fell into the hands of King Alcinous (later Ulysses' host) who, after hearing their story, decreed that the maid Medea must be returned to her father. But before Alcinous could act on this sentence, Jason married Medea, so that she was no longer the *maid* Medea, and in this way Jason and Medea evaded justice. On their way to Greece, they were driven by a storm onto the Syrtes. Delivered by Hera and Poseidon, they arrived at Lake Tritonis.

Here they could not find the channel which would bring them to the Mediterranean, until Triton, whose lake this was, guided them through the shallows to a channel near Cyrene. Before parting company with them, Triton gave to Euphemus a clod of earth from Cyrene. Medea by her magic revealed the secret that if Euphemus would throw this clod into the cavern at Taenarum (the entrance to the Lower World through which Hercules had dragged Cerberus), his descendants in the tenth generation would become the masters of Cyrene.

The Argonauts would have landed in Crete but Medea warned them of the giant robot Talus, who appeared at that moment and began to throw boulders at the ship. With a magic spell Medea caused the plug in his ankle to fall out. He lost the fluid which animated him and became forever motionless. Alarmed by their narrow escape, the Argonauts put in at Thera instead of Crete. Here Euphemus lost his precious clod. As a result his descendants became masters only of Thera and it was not until the seventeenth generation that one of them left Thera to colonize Cyrene.

From Thera the *Argo* reached Iolcus safely. But during Jason's absence Pelias had assassinated Jason's father and brother, and his mother had killed herself. In order to avenge these deaths, Medea by the following device tricked the daughters of Pelias into killing their father. As they looked on, she cut up an aged he-goat and boiled the pieces in a cauldron with magical herbs, whereupon the goat leapt out of the pot rejuvenated. They, of course, wanted to perform the same service for their aged father and asked Medea for the magical herbs. She pretended to agree, but gave them worthless ones. Instead of a rejuvenated father, they ended up with a particularly nasty kind of soup. This event outraged the people of Iolcus and, led by Pelias' son, Jason's erstwhile friend Acastus, they drove Jason and Medea from the land. The fugitives took refuge in Corinth where they had two sons.

In Iolcus Jason had had some hope of gaining his father's throne, but in Corinth he was only a private citizen. And, in civilized Greece, his barbaric foreign wife began to be a social embarrassment to him. Also, reflecting on her treachery to her father, her murder of her brother, and the trick she played on the daughters of Pelias, he may have felt some misgivings, even though these deeds had all been done for him. So when Creon, the King of Corinth, offered the distinguished foreigner his daughter Glauce's hand in marriage, Jason accepted and Creon pronounced a sentence of banishment upon Medea.

At this point King Aegeus of Athens passed through Corinth. He was on his way from Delphi (where he had consulted the oracle about his childlessness) to Troezen to consult his old friend King Pittheus about Apollo's puzzling response. By promising to cure his childlessness with her spells, Medea induced him to swear that if she ever came to him as a suppliant he would refuse to give her up to her enemies. He did not know her dreadful plans. First she sent as a wedding present to Creon's daughter Glauce a poisoned robe and wreath. When Glauce put them on, they clung to her flesh and then burst into flames, and when Creon tried to save her they were both burnt alive. Medea then murdered both of her and Jason's sons before his eyes. Then, mounting a chariot drawn by flying dragons which had been sent for her by her grandfather, the Sun, she flew off to Athens. Her doings there have been described in the comments on *Theseus and the Minotaur*, Lesson 10.

Medea later was reconciled with her father and returned to Colchis where her son by Aegeus, Medus, became the ancestor of the Medes. Jason had dedicated the *Argo* to Poseidon and set it up on the shore of the Isthmus of Corinth. One day while he was resting in its shade the stern fell off and killed him.

Medea is one of the most complex characters of ancient literature, inspiring both sympathy as a betrayed and deserted heroine, and repulsion as a witch and murderess. She is usually portrayed as coming from a less civilized background than her husband. The Colchians are symbols of cold-blooded cruelty in the literature, so that the acts which shock the more sophisticated and hypocritical Greeks seem natural to her. Her character, particularly as portrayed by Euripides and Apollonius, has entered into the imagination of western literature so that, aside from the many works written about Medea herself, the figure of the simple untutored child of nature who doesn't understand why she should not live by her own less civilized code, or that of the foreign wife unable to adapt to her husband's background, is familiar in countless modern plays and novels. Your students might like to identify some of these.

They might also like to find and identify in the story of Jason the numerous elements of folk tale, using an unabridged edition of the Grimm brothers' collection of *Maerchen*, the *Household Tales*, in which such themes as those of the Ogre's Daughter and the Talented Companions occur again and again. Such themes appear in many a myth, but in no other do they have so pervasive an underlying influence.

PRACTICAL APPLICATIONS

_____ Specific Literary References _____

1. Chiron, the wisest of the Centaurs, and the only immortal one, rests on Mt. Pelion in Thessaly, the homeland of the Centaurs.

2. The straits between the Aegean and the Propontis (Sea of Marmora), so named ("Sea of Helle") because Helle fell into these straits from the back of the flying golden ram.

3. Jason's ship, so called after its builder, Argus, son of Phrixus; from it the Argonauts, "Argo Sailors" took their name.

4. When there was no wind or an adverse wind, and the Argonauts were tired of rowing, Orpheus caused the ship to move through the water by the spell of his songs.

5. The hideous bird-women who snatched Phineus' food away before he could eat it.

6. A reference to Helle's fall from the back of the golden ram which was carrying her and her brother Phrixus to safety.

7. Hylas was Hercules' beloved page [whom he had taken with him after he had killed his father in a fight].

8. In some accounts Hercules (Herakles) finds the drowned body of Hylas and gives it a funeral. [More often he leaves after ordering the Mysians to continue the search, which Apollonius says they were still doing in his day (IIId Century B.C.)].

_____ Word Study _____

1. The Nineteenth Century, a time when a classical education was more common than it is today, naturally saw the similarity between the Argonauts in search of the Golden Fleece and those who traveled so far (usually by ship) to seek the gold of California.

2. Nestor lived to a ripe old age, his life span bridging the time between the pre-Trojan War generation of heroes (he took part, for example, in the Calydonian Boar Hunt) and the Trojan War in which he fought. He was still alive and healthy ten years after the war, having ruled over three generations of men. In the *Iliad* he is a respected senior, and the kings value his advice (though this may be a piece of sly humor on Homer's part, since his advice is usually ineffectual or irrelevant).

4. The Greeks have always called themselves "Hellenes" and their country "Hellas." The word applied to them by the rest of the world is owed to the accident that the first Greek whom the Italians met happened to be a Graean, part of a minority among the colonizers of Cumae near Naples. From *Graios* Latin made the adjective *Graecus*, and so gave the word "Greek" to the world. The Hellenes themselves thought that their name came from their common ancestor Hellen, a son of Deucalion, two of whose sons, Dorus and Aeolus (not the King of the Winds), were the ancestors of the Dorians and Aeolians. The third son, Xuthus, himself had two sons, Ion and Achaeus, the ancestors of the Ionians and the Achaeans. In other words, the Greeks, in spite of their differences, recognized that they had a common ancestry. They rigidly excluded peoples like the Macedonians who, in spite of having the same languages and religion, could not show descent from Hellen. "Hellenic" is a more pedantic way of saying "Greek." The Hellespont lies between the Aegean and the Sea of Marmora. Since the word means "Sea of Helle," the Greeks explained that it had been so named from Helle's falling into it when she lost her seat on the flying golden ram.

1. Aeson.

2. He resigned his throne in his favor on condition that he yield it to Aeson's son Jason when he should come of age.

3. He went to Iolcus to claim his throne.

4. By sending him on a quest for the Golden Fleece.

5. He went to fetch the Golden Fleece from Colchis.

6. He summoned the heroes of Greece to accompany him.

7. *Argo.*

8. [Acastus,] Admetus, [Amphiaraus, Ancaeus,] Arcas, Argus, Atalanta, [Butes,] Calais, Castor, [Erginus, Euphemus,] Hercules, [Idas, Idmon, Lynceus, Meleager, Mopsus,] Nestor, Orpheus, Peleus, [Periclymenus,] Pollux, Telamon, Theseus, [Tiphys, Tydeus,] Zetes [and twenty-four others].

9. He stayed behind [in Mysia] to search for his page Hylas, who had been stolen by water-nymphs.

10. By boxing with and killing a king [King Amycus of the Bebryces].

11. By driving away the Harpies who had been stealing his food; he explained how to pass safely between the Symplegades.

12. By sending a dove to fly through first; the Symplegades caught its tail, but the time it took them to rebound and come together again gave the *Argo* time to slip through [though she did lose her rudder].

13. That he yoke the fire-breathing bulls of Ares, plow a field with them, and sow the dragon's teeth.

14. Aeetes' daughter Medea.

15. By means of a magical ointment which Medea gave him.

16. By throwing a stone among them, thus provoking them to fight and kill each other.

17. Medea gave it a drug in its food which put it to sleep.

18. He was killed by his own daughters through a trick of Medea's.

19. He dedicated it to Poseidon [setting it up on the shore of the Isthmus of Corinth].

13   The Trojan War

Judgment of Paris

Before giving birth to Paris, Hecuba dreamed that she had given birth to a firebrand which set fire to the city; this is why he was exposed on Mt. Ida. This practice of "exposure" was the Greek method of getting rid of unwanted children. It protected the parents from the blood-guilt of actually killing the child. (We have already seen it practiced in the myths of Oedipus and Perseus.) It was a real custom which continued into historical times, though in later, more civilized settings, the baby was not taken into the wilds but was left in a kind of pound, whence anyone wanting a slave to train or a child to adopt could take it home. Some identification in the form of a locket or the like could be left with the child, so that the parents could later buy it back if they changed their minds.

Later versions of the myth present Paris as a connoisseur of female beauty. In the original story, however, he must have been chosen because (though he was of royal birth and hence worthy to look upon the unclothed goddesses) his life in the wilds had kept him unspoilt and unprejudiced.

Leda was a sister of Althea, the mother of Meleager, and was married to King Tyndareus of Sparta. Having been visited by both Zeus (in the form of a swan) and her husband in the same night, she eventually gave birth to two babies, Castor and Clytemnestra, Tyndareus' children, and at the same time laid an egg from which hatched Pollux and Helen, the children of Zeus. The eggshell was still being shown to tourists at Sparta in the IId Century of our era. Divine-human superfetation is not rare in the myths. We have seen it in the case of Hercules and Iphicles. It was because Tyndareus had on one occasion neglected to sacrifice to Aphrodite that she caused both of the daughters to grow up to be notorious adulteresses.

As we have seen, even as a young child Helen had already been abducted once by Theseus and rescued by her brothers.

When Menelaus married Helen, his brother Agamemnon married her sister Clytemnestra. When Castor and Pollux died and became semi-immortal (Zeus granted Pollux' request that he share his immortality with his mortal brother, so that they took turns being dead on alternate days), Tyndareus gave his throne to Menelaus, so that at the time of the War he and his brother were the Kings of Sparta and Mycenae (or in some versions Argos).

By the time of his journey to Sparta, Paris had married Oenone, the daughter of a river-god. He had also become a leader of the herdsmen among whom he lived and had been given by them the name Alexander, "Protector of Men," by which he is sometimes called. He had also become, in the process of protecting his flocks, very proficient in archery

On one occasion Priam, who had come to regret the loss of Paris, was celebrating funeral games in memory of his (supposedly) dead son. He sent his servants to bring the best bull from his herds to sacrifice. The bull which they chose was one which had been a pet of Paris. Although Paris knew nothing of cities and their life, he determined to go to Troy and rescue it. Once arrived, he innocently decided to take part in the games, not realizing that a simple herdsman was not supposed to join in these aristocratic sports. He defeated all his brothers, even Hector, in archery. Enraged at the presumption of this rustic, they were going to kill him. But when Cassandra, who by her prophetic powers recognized him and foresaw the destruction he was to bring upon Troy, urged them on, they of course desisted, since Cassandra's advice was never followed. Priam recognized Paris as his son and so Paris never returned to his flocks. Life in the city soon made him forget poor Oenone and he was very willing, when Aphrodite summoned him, to go and fetch Helen.

Gathering the Hosts

Ulysses' mother Anticleia was the daughter of Autolycus, a son of Hermes. Autolycus was known as the best wrestler of his day (he had been Hercules' tutor) and also the cleverest thief; only Sisyphus ever bested him. But Ulysses surpassed his grandfather in wiliness and deviousness; some said that Sisyphus, and not Laertes, was Ulysses' real father.

Ulysses' only rival in ingenuity and cleverness was Palamedes, son of King Nauplius of Euboea. Palamedes had added four more letters to the alphabet which Cadmus had brought from Phoenicia; he was the inventor of the lighthouse and of standardized weights and measures. To while away the weary time at war, he also invented dice and the game of checkers.

Ulysses already felt some jealousy toward Palamedes, but when Palamedes detected his pretence of insanity he became his implacable enemy. Once at Troy, Ulysses brought about his death by a plot. Having forged a letter from Priam, he concealed it along with a sum of gold under Palamedes' bed. He then spread rumors that Palamedes was a traitor. Palamedes' tent was searched, the planted evidence was found, and the army stoned him to death.

When Nauplius heard of his son's death, he built false lighthouses along the Euboean coast and lit fires in them when the Greeks were returning from Troy. This caused the shipwreck and death of many a Greek; in this way he got his revenge.

Thetis in some of the stories is like the mermaid-wife of folk tales. When the *Argo*, the first ship ever to cleave the waters, set sail, Thetis and her sister Nereids rose from the water to see this marvel; it was then that she and Peleus fell in love. After their marriage, knowing that her marriage to a mortal condemned her child to mortality, Thetis secretly anointed the infant Achilles nightly with ambrosia and placed him in the fire to burn away his mortal parts (compare the story of Demeter and Demophoon). Her plans were thwarted when Peleus came upon her unexpectedly and snatched the baby from the flames. In her anger she deserted her husband and child and returned to the sea, pausing only to dip the baby in the Styx in order to make him at least invulnerable.

Achilles' land of Phthia owed no fealty to Agamemnon, nor was Achilles bound by the oath the other heroes had taken. Thetis knew however that once Achilles learned his fate, that he could choose either to die young at Troy after achieving great glory or have a long but inglorious life at home, he would choose death and glory. She hid him among the daughters of King Lycomedes of Scyrus (the murderer of Theseus) for two reasons: to keep knowledge of the war from him and to conceal him from the chieftains, who would try to enlist his aid once they learned that Troy could not be taken without him. It is a poignant sequel to Achilles' choice that when Ulysses later meets him among the Dead he appears to regret it. When Ulysses calls him the luckiest man who ever lived, having had a life full of glory and being now a mighty ruler among the Dead, Achilles contradicts him, saying, "I would rather be a slave on earth to a poor man with no land than be king of all the Dead."

While on Scyrus Achilles begot, by Lycomedes' daughter Deidamia, his only son Pyrrhus who came to fight at Troy after his father's death. He was given the name Neoptolemus, "New to War."

There were other prophecies concerning the fall of Troy besides the one which required the presence of Achilles. Delphi had been consulted and had said that Troy would fall when the best of the Greeks quarreled. Calchas, the prophet of the Greek armies, knew that it could not fall so long as it retained the *Palladium*, a wooden image of Athena which had fallen from heaven in the time of Ilus, the grandfather of Priam. When the Greeks were about to set sail from Aulis, they were making a sacrifice under a tree when a snake came from under the altar and climbed the tree. There it found a bird's nest, ate the eight fledglings and their mother and then was turned to stone. Calchas explained that this meant Troy would hold out for nine years, then fall in the tenth.

War Against Troy

Achilles brought his fifty ships to the war separately from the rest of the expedition and, landing in Asia Minor, took twenty-three towns, in most cases killing their men, but taking the women for slaves. At Thebe in Cilicia, he killed King Eetion and his seven sons, the father and brothers of Andromache, the wife of Hector. Among the women whom he enslaved were Briseis, daughter of Briseus of Lyrnessus, and Chryseis, daughter of Chryses, a priest of the town of Chryse. He also took much booty which he generously shared with the other kings on his arrival at Troy. He also distributed his new slaves to his allies (giving Chryseis to Agamemnon), but kept Briseis for himself.

In the course of his campaigns in Asia Minor Achilles fought with Hercules' son Telephus. The mother of Telephus was Auge, a daughter of King Aleus of Tegea and sister of Hercules' ally King Cepheus. Because Auge was a priestess of Athena, the land had been punished with failures of crops, and Aleus was warned by Delphi to destroy his daughter and grandson. He gave them to Nauplius of Euboea to kill but Nauplius exposed the baby and gave Auge to King Teuthras of Mysia. When Telephus grew up he consulted Delphi about his parentage and was directed to Mysia, where Teuthras welcomed him and bequeathed him his throne. As a son of Hercules he might have been a match for Achilles, but Dionysus caused him to trip over a vine and Achilles wounded him in the thigh. The wound would not heal and when on another pilgrimage to Delphi he learned that only the weapon which had caused the wound could heal it, he went as a suppliant to Agamemnon, who persuaded Achilles to rub the wound with the rust of his spearhead. Thus cured, Telephus became a friend to the Greeks, even though he was married to a sister of Priam. His son Eurypylus fought on the Trojan side in the last year of the war and was killed by Pyrrhus.

Ancient writers all agree that the Trojan War lasted ten years; yet they also tell us that its first battle took place in the tenth year. In fact, all the reported events of the war (except for the medieval story of Troilus and Cressida), occurred in the final year. In his story of the tenth year, Homer even has Priam ask Helen to point out for him, from the walls of Troy, the chief Greek leaders, whom he surely should have known by that time. It seems most likely that the war (which most historians now believe to have been an actual event) was much shorter, but was eventually made into a ten years' war to emphasize its importance. It is the chief event of the last part of the Heroic Age, surpassing in its scope and repercussions such earlier gatherings of heroes as the Calydonian Boar Hunt and the Voyage of the Argonauts.

The quarrel between Agamemnon and Achilles arose in the following way. Chryseis' father Chryses came to Agamemnon to ransom his daughter. Agamemnon, who had become fond of his slave, refused; so Apollo, resenting this insult to his priest, sent a plague onto the Greek camp. Calchas revealed that the only cure was the restoration of Chryseis. Having sent her back to her father, Agamemnon felt that it was unseemly that he, the Commander-in-Chief, should be without a slave; consequently he demanded that Achilles give Briseis to him. Prevented by Athena from killing Agamemnon, Achilles yielded but refused thereafter to fight.

Stratagem of the Wooden Horse

Homer's account of the war, which begins with the quarrel, ends with the funeral games of Hector, but other authors carry on the story for us. Upon the death of Hector the Amazons came to the aid of Troy, but their queen, Penthesilea, was killed in single combat by Achilles and they returned home. Priam's nephew Memnon brought an Ethiopian army but he also fell to Achilles.

Apollo's prophecy that Troy would fall after the best of the Greeks had quarreled, began to be fulfilled when Ulysses and Achilles argued bitterly at a banquet about the best way to take Troy. Achilles argued that it could be done by fighting fearlessly, Ulysses that trickery would be needed.

Despairing of victory, the Trojans arranged for a peace treaty, to be confirmed by the marriage of Polyxena (a daughter of Priam and Hecuba) to Achilles. The wedding, at the temple of Apollo outside the walls of Troy, was disrupted by the death of Achilles, whom Paris shot in the heel with a poisoned arrow. He aimed from a great distance, the top of the walls, but he was the best archer of his day. Besides that, the arrow was guided by Apollo.

After the death of Achilles the sides were again evenly matched, but the capture of Helenus by Ulysses marked another turning point. Helenus, a son of Priam and Hecuba, was a seer. Knowing the threat that Helen posed to his fatherland, he had wanted to send her back, but succumbed to her fatal beauty and fell in love with her. When her hand was awarded to his brother Deiphobus, he decided in his chagrin to retire to Mt. Ida. On the way he fell into the hands of Ulysses who hoped that he would be able to tell the Greeks how Troy might be taken at last. He revealed to them that they could not succeed without the arrows of Hercules by which Troy had fallen in the First Trojan War and without the help of a descendant of Achilles.

Hercules, on his funeral pyre, had given his famous poisoned arrows to Poeas, King of the Malians, in whose land the pyre was built. Poeas' son

Philoctetes, one of Helen's suitors, had inherited the arrows. Philoctetes was bringing seven ships to the war. He stopped to take on water on the island of Chryse and was bitten by a snake. He did not die of the bite but the wound refused to heal and emitted such a foul smell that no one could come near him. Accordingly, on the advice of Ulysses, the Greeks marooned him on the island of Lemnos. Ulysses was now faced with the delicate task of persuading the embittered Philoctetes to bring the arrows to Troy. With the help of Diomedes he succeeded and they brought Philoctetes from Lemnos. Philoctetes was the greatest archer of his time, better even than Paris, and he killed many Greeks, Paris among them. Wounded by Philoctetes' arrow, Paris returned to Oenone, who had the power to heal him, but she, resentful of his infidelity, refused, and he died. She then repented and killed herself.

The second requirement was easily satisfied by bringing Achilles' son Pyrrhus (now to be called Neoptolemus) from Scyrus to Troy.

With the theft of the Palladium all the ordained conditions were fulfilled and Troy was at last ripe to fall. Ulysses, in disguise, had visited Helen in Troy and received her assurance that she would aid the Greeks. While Sinon was opening the Horse to let the warriors out, she stood upon the walls of Troy and signaled with a torch to the Greek fleet. She then led her husband Menelaus to the house of her husband Deiphobus who, taken unawares, died after Menelaus cut off his nose and ears.

Many horrors are related of the night that Troy fell. The Greek armies released upon the city the pent-up fury of ten years, burning, killing, and plundering indiscriminately. Old Priam, when he understood what had happened, girt on his rusty armor to fight, but Hecuba drew him to join her at their household altar of Zeus, along with their daughter Polyxena. To the altar came running Polites, their youngest son, pursued by Pyrrhus, who killed the defenseless boy in his mother's arms. Outraged, the aged Priam threw his spear at Pyrrhus but the feeble blow did no damage. Pyrrhus seized the king by the hair, dragged his head back over the altar, and cut his throat as his wife and daughter looked on.

Cassandra, pursued by Ajax (the son of Oileus, not the greater hero, Ajax the son of Telamon), took refuge in the temple of Athena, clasping the feet of the goddess' statue. Ajax tore her from the temple, overturning the statue.

Living in a more remote part of the city, Aeneas was not awakened by the clamor, but was visited in a dream by the ghost of his brother-in-law Hector, which warned him to assemble his family and flee, since it was now too late to save Troy. Aeneas' first thought was to die with Troy and he rushed to the center of the city. But after killing many Greeks, he thought of his family, returned, and escaped with them.

In the morning the Greeks herded together the women and children of Troy to wait while their captors drew lots to see whose slave each would be. But they were interrupted by the terrifying appearance of the ghost of Achilles, demanding to have his share in this booty. He required that Polyxena, whom he was to have married, be sacrificed on his tomb.

Even after Neoptolemus had slaughtered Polyxena on his father's tomb, one more Trojan death was required. Calchas revealed that the gods would not send the Greeks a favorable wind until Astyanax, Hector's young son, was thrown to his death from the top of the only tower left standing in Troy. His mother Andromache tried to save him by hiding him in Hector's tomb; but unluckily Ulysses, in trying to force her to reveal the child's hiding place, threatened to level the tomb if she didn't tell. Seeing that Astyanax would be doomed in any case, she turned him over to Odysseus and he was hurled from the tower by the implacable Neoptolemus.

The allotment now proceeded: Cassandra fell to the lot of Agamemnon; Andromache was given to Neoptolemus, the son of the man who had killed her father, brothers, and husband; and Ulysses received the aged Hecuba for his slave.

A victory banquet was now held to decide who was to receive the divinely made arms of Achilles. Thetis had required that they be given to the hero most responsible for the fall of Troy. The chief claimants were Ajax son of Telamon, the bravest and strongest of the heroes after Achilles, and Ulysses, who had performed no great feats of valor but had devised the stratagem of the horse. When the voting reached a deadlock, the few surviving Trojans were made to vote and the armor was awarded to Ulysses. This slight was too much for Ajax who went mad and attempted to kill the other Greek kings; in his madness he slaughtered a flock of sheep instead. When he came to himself and saw what he had done, he committed suicide.

PRACTICAL APPLICATIONS

_____ Specific Literary References _____

1. Achilles, insulted by having had to relinquish his slave to Agamemnon, refused to leave his tent.

2. Thais, literally setting fire to Persepolis (see Plutarch's *Life of Alexander*) is compared to Helen whose beauty was responsible for the burning of Troy, "the face that . . . burnt the topless towers of Ilium."

3. Andromache, daughter of Eetion of Thebe, wife of Hector, and mother of Astyanax.

4. Nestor of Pylus was the oldest of the heroes at Troy, having reigned over three generations of men.

5. King Priam of Troy, one of whose fifty sons was Paris.

6. Ate was the goddess of Discord, the one who threw the golden apple at the wedding of Peleus and Thetis.

7. It took the Greeks ten years of perseverance to enter the city.

8. The reference is to Achilles' pursuit of Hector around the walls of Troy.

_____ Word Study _____

2. No; it derives rather from the character of Hector as he appears in medieval romances about the Trojan War. Hector is a sympathetic character in both Homer and Virgil.

3. The *Myrmidons* were Achilles' faithful followers, who withdrew from the war and then fought again when he ordered them to. Achilles' grandfather Aeacus, finding himself the king of the unpopulated island of Aegina, had asked Zeus to create a people for him from the ants (Greek *myrmeces*), and Zeus had done so, making the first Myrmidons. The Arcadian *Stentor*, one of the Greek heroes at Troy, could shout as loud as fifty men together; he later died as a result of a shouting contest with Hermes.

4. In anatomy the *Achilles' tendon* is the one that runs up the back of the heel, a reference to the vulnerability of Achilles' heel. *Ulysses* was the wiliest of the heroes, as is abundantly illustrated by the myths concerning him. Because of his seniority *Nestor* had a reputation (apparently unjustified) for wisdom. *Paris' judgment* was difficult because (as he must have known) any choice he made would gain him the enmity of two powerful goddesses. *Achilles' sulking* in his tent is almost the entire subject of the *Iliad*. *Like a Trojan* means "showing courage and endurance," from the Trojans' ability to sustain a ten-years' siege. *The Apple of Discord* was the golden apple inscribed "for the fairest" which the goddess of Discord threw into the wedding feast of Peleus and Thetis.

_____ Questions for Review _____

1. There was an oracle that her son would be greater than his father.

2. The Argonaut King Peleus [of Phthia, son of Aeacus].

3. Ate, or Eris.

4. She threw a golden apple, inscribed "for the fairest," into the midst of the festivities.

5. In favor of Aphrodite.

6. Priam; Troy.

7. Queen Helen of Sparta.

8. That all of them should help whichever won her to keep her.

9. Menelaus.

10. Aided by Aphrodite, he persuaded Helen to elope with him.

11. He called upon the kings to honor their oath.

12. Ulysses, happily married and with an infant son, didn't want to leave home.

13. He was pretending madness, plowing with an ox and ass yoked together and sowing salt; but Palamedes placed the infant Telemachus in front of the plow and he revealed his sanity by turning the plow aside.

14. The son of Peleus and Thetis.

15. That his life would be short and glorious or long and inglorious.

16. Ulysses.

17. Agamemnon had killed a stag which was a pet of Artemis; she arranged for adverse winds.

18. By the sacrifice of Agamemnon's daughter Iphigenia.

19. Practically nothing.

20. Over a division of the spoils of war: [Agamemnon demanded that Achilles yield to him Briseis, part of Achilles' booty].

21. Achilles sulked in his tent and refused to fight or to let his Myrmidons do so.

22. He persuaded Achilles to let him borrow his armor and lead the Myrmidons to battle. Hector killed him, supposing that he was Achilles.

23. Bitter grief and burning anger.

24. In a hand-to-hand contest with Achilles he turned and ran; Achilles pursued and killed him.

25. Paris shot Achilles in his vulnerable heel with a poisoned arrow;

Paris was shot [by Philoctetes] with a poisoned arrow [one of Hercules'].

26.   A hollow wooden horse was built, big enough to contain some of the Greek kings and too big to enter the city without the demolition of part of the wall; the Greeks were persuaded by Sinon that it was an offering to Athena which would bring good fortune to Troy if it were brought into the city. At night the men inside were released [by Sinon] and joined by the rest of the fleet.

27.   Laocoon.

28.   He was devoured, along with his two sons, by two serpents from the sea.

29.   It was taken and destroyed.

_____ Reading List _____

Christopher Morley's serio-comic novel, *The Trojan Horse*, is set in Troy at the time of the war. Playing upon the fact that the Trojan War has fascinated all ages, including our own, Morley amusingly mixes ancient, medieval, and modern details, having Priam give the Trojan warriors a football-coach style pep-talk in the locker room at half-time, making Cassandra an Economics major in horn-rimmed spectacles, and so on. There are some scenes of sexual activity in the book; you will want to read it before deciding whether school policy will allow you to recommend it.

14   After the Trojan War

Return of the Heroes

The Greeks had not punished Ajax son of Oileus for his profanation of Athena's temple when he seized Cassandra. In retaliation she persuaded Poseidon to disperse their fleet with a storm, so that each of the kings returned home by a different route. Some, like Menelaus and Ulysses, were a long time in their homecoming. Some were wrecked on the rocks of Euboea, misled by the false beacons of Palamedes' father Nauplius. Some, like Diomedes and Pyrrhus (Neoptolemus), although they survived, never reached home. Ajax himself was pierced by a thunderbolt of Jove, hurled by Minerva's own hand, and cast from his ship. Undaunted, he swam to a nearby rock; but when he boasted that even the gods could not destroy him, Neptune shattered the rock with his trident, and Ajax drowned.

During the storm King Idomeneus of Crete (Minos' grandson) vowed to Poseidon that if he were saved he would sacrifice to him the first living thing he saw when he had come safely home. This proved to be his own son. (Compare the story of Jephthah's daughter in the Old Testament.) The sacrifice so displeased the gods that a plague broke out in Crete, and Idomeneus was banished; he went to Calabria in Italy.

Philoctetes also eventually ended up in Italy. Having escaped the storm, he arrived home safely; but he was still so embittered by his treatment at the hands of his fellow Greeks that he went to Italy and founded the city of Petelia on the shores of the Adriatic.

During the war Diomedes had on one occasion wounded Aphrodite herself, who had been incautious enough to take the field on the Trojan side. To punish him she tempted his wife Aegiale into adultery. Learning of this and of the fate of Agamemnon, he did not return to Argos but headed for his grandfather's home in Aetolia. From here he was driven by a storm to the shores of Apulia in Italy. Having married the king's daughter, he eventually became King of Apulia. When he heard that Aeneas had settled in Italy, he sent him the Palladium of Troy, which in after years was kept in a secret compartment of the Temple of Vesta in Rome. In later years Diomedes disappeared while on a sea voyage to the Adriatic islands, afterwards called the Islands of Diomedes. His companions were metamorphosed into herons.

Menelaus and Helen, accompanied by Nestor, were among the first to leave Troy. They escaped the storm stirred up by Poseidon, but later, rounding Cape Malea, were driven southward to Egypt. They wandered for eight years there and in adjoining lands. They were hospitably received wherever they went, but prevented by the gods from returning home because Menelaus had failed to make the proper sacrifices. At last, kept on the island of Pharos near Egypt by contrary winds, Menelaus was met by the sea-nymph Eidothea, daughter of Proteus. She took pity on him and explained how he could find out which god was detaining him. She said that at noon her father would emerge from the sea, accompanied by the seals, who would fall asleep on the island. He would count them and then go to sleep himself. To enable Menelaus to catch him, she fetched from the sea four fresh sealskins to serve as disguises for Menelaus and three companions, even thoughtfully rubbing their nostrils with ambrosia to disguise the terrible smell. When Proteus had fallen asleep, Menelaus and his men seized him and held on while he turned himself into a lion, a snake, a panther, a boar, running water, and a tree. He then capitulated and agreed to answer Menelaus' questions, instructing him to return to Egypt and there to sacrifice to all the gods. In response to further questions, he also told Menelaus of the deaths of Ajax and Agamemnon and of Ulysses' detention on Ogygia. He further prophesied that Menelaus, by virtue of being Helen's husband, would not die but would come alive to the Islands of the Blest. Having returned to Egypt and having made the proper sacrifices, Menelaus was granted an easy voyage home.

When he left Troy, Neoptolemus (Pyrrhus) was accompanied by his captives, Andromache and her brother-in-law, the seer Helenus. Helenus warned Neoptolemus that it would be dangerous for him to return to Scyrus or to go to his paternal grandfather's kingdom of Phthia. Instead he sailed around to Epirus on the west coast of the Balkan Peninsula. Here he became king. The famous Pyrrhus of Epirus, kinsman of Alexander the Great, traced his descent and took his name from him. His son by Andromache, Molossus, became the ancestor of the Molossians.

The danger of which Helenus had warned Neoptolemus did not fall upon him until he visited Phthia to restore his grandfather Peleus to his throne, from which he had been driven by the king of Iolcus. Having succeeded in this, he married Hermione, daughter of Menelaus and Helen. However, on a visit to Delphi he was killed by her cousin Orestes to whom she had been betrothed. The betrothal was broken off when Orestes killed his mother, Helen's sister. He killed Neoptolemus during the time when he was wandering maddened and pursued by the furies. Since Neoptolemus was killed at the very altar of Apollo, it was clear that this was a just retribution for his slaying of Priam at the altar of Zeus.

Upon Neoptolemus' death Andromache married Helenus and together they ruled over Chaonia, the northern part of Epirus. Hermione was married to Orestes after he had been cured of his madness and purified from his blood-guilt.

This was not accomplished until he came to Athens where he was tried for the murder of his mother before the court of the Areopagus (the same legal body which was later to hear St. Paul's exposition of the Christian faith). Athena as Goddess of Athens was judge, the Furies prosecuted, and Apollo, who at Delphi had laid upon Orestes the necessity of avenging his father's murder, spoke for the defense. The jury was divided, but Athena, never very sympathetic with mothers since she neither was nor had one herself, cast the deciding vote and Orestes was acquitted and cured. The Furies, mollified by the offer of a sanctuary at Athens, accepted the new name of Eumenides, "Well-Wishers".

Adventures of Ulysses

According to later stories, but not the *Odyssey*, Ulysses' first stop after leaving Troy was in Thrace, in the kingdom of Polymnestor. This king had married Ilione, a daughter of Priam and Hecuba. When the fall of Troy seemed near, Priam had sent to Ilione his son Polydorus with some of the most valuable treasures of Troy for safekeeping. When Polymnestor heard that Troy had fallen, he killed Polydorus in order to keep the treasures for himself. When Hecuba, who had accompanied Ulysses to Thrace as his captive, learned of this, she flew at Polymnestor and scratched out his eyes. Then, as she railed at him, she was metamorphosed into a barking dog and jumped into the sea from a headland which was thereafter known as Cynossema ("Dog's Monument"), an important landmark for mariners.

It is clear that Homer had little or no knowledge of geography outside the shores of the Aegean. When Ulysses rounded Cape Malea at the southern end of the Peloponnesus, he sailed off the map into a mythical area. Any attempt to reconcile times, distances, and directions with the ·geography of the Mediterranean meets with insurmountable difficulties. Yet as soon as the Greek world started to acquire first-hand knowledge of the western Mediterranean, the practice of "identifying" the places visited by Ulysses began. The Cyclopes were placed in Sicily, Scylla and Charybdis at the Straits of Messina, the land of the Phaeacians in Corcyra (Corfu), and so on, so that by the time of Virgil many of these places had become a part of the real geography of the Mediterranean. The practice continues into our own day, as enthusiasts sail around the Mediterranean watching for Homeric landmarks, then write books or make films to prove that the "true" route of Ulysses has at last been found. This makes about as much sense as an attempt to prove that the Emerald City was "really" Samarkand.

It is possible of couse that Homer, living (as we suppose) in Ionia, wove into his story travelers' tales received at second or third hand. By the earliest date which can seriously be assigned to him the Phoenicians had already explored the western Mediterranean. This premise is taken up by *Lands Beyond*, a book about the imaginary geographies of various works of literature. This book is becoming hard to find but is still in many libraries. The authors, Willy Ley and L. Sprague Decamp, never lose sight of the imaginary nature of the various locales, but do speculate interestingly and convincingly on the possible origins, in the real adventures of early sailors, of the places visited by Ulysses.

In spite of its early date, the *Odyssey* is one of the most masterfully told tales of all time. Its characters come to life in a way that is rare in literature, ancient or modern. In fact, they are so vividly portrayed that they almost seem to have a life which is independent of the work in which they appear, so that one finds it difficult to think of them as fictional. Even the monstrous Polyphemus is given a real personality, even a sympathetic one. In his speech to his pet ram, which is moving slowly because it is weighed down by Ulysses, in which he asks it if it is going so slowly out of pity for its master's blindness, he wins our sympathy even while we are hoping that he won't think of the real reason. This vividness is found in very few works of Western fiction. One thinks of some of Shakespeare's characters, some of Dickens', Sherlock Holmes, but not many more. The mere outline of the story which is all that there is space for in a text of this scope cannot convey this vivid quality, nor is there room for the sub-plots: Penelope's own cleverness in her struggle to maintain the kingship of Ithaca intact until the return of her husband or the majority of her son, and the "Telemachy," Telemachus' adventures in search of his father.

The deviousness of Ulysses, who devises the most elaborate lies when simple ones, or none, would do, and his demonstrable lack of success as a leader still do not prevent him from being one of the most sympathetic characters in fiction. Virgil goes out of his way to show us that Aeneas has none of Ulysses' dishonesty and rashness; but Aeneas has never inspired in the readers of his story the love which most feel for Ulysses. Your students should certainly be urged to read the *Odyssey*.

While in Hades Ulysses was told by Tiresias that, in order to appease the wrath of Poseidon, once he had returned home he was to set out again with a steering oar. He was to travel until he came to a place where salt was unknown and where the people would mistake the oar for a winnowing fan. There he was to sacrifice to Poseidon, thus bringing his worship to a land necessarily far from the sea. After this, death would come to him "from the sea."

A later epic, the *Telegonia*, now lost, told of the end of Ulysses. Ulysses made the pilgrimage enjoined on him by Tiresias and then returned to Ithaca, which he found being plundered by a young invader. This was actually Telegonus, his son by Circe, who had been sent by his mother in search of his father, armed by her with a magical spear tipped with the poisonous barb of a sting-ray. Father and son failed to recognize each other and in their fight Ulysses died, poisoned by the sting-ray barb; this was his death from the sea. Too late Telegonus learned that this was his father. He returned to Aeaea, taking with him Penelope and Telemachus. There Circe granted immortality and eternal youth to all three and they lived there ever after, Telemachus having married Circe and Telegonus Penelope.

PRACTICAL APPLICATIONS

_____ Specific Literary References _____

1. Cassandra was one of the fifty daughters of Priam; she had been granted by Apollo the gift of prophecy, accompanied by the curse that her prophecies would never be believed.

2. Odysseus' faithful dog waited twenty years for his return, then died when he had greeted him.

3. For eight years Odysseus was a prisoner of Calypso, who wanted him to marry her.

4. Odysseus throws off his disguise as a beggar and prepares to shoot with his great bow.

5. A reference to Ulysses' device for hearing the song of the Sirens without perishing: he deafened his crew by putting wax in their ears and had himself tied to the mast, not trusting himself not to leap overboard.

6. Ulysses entered the Lower World twice, once to visit the prophet Tiresias and once when he died.

7. A reference to Circe's powers as an enchantress.

8. A reference to the bag in which Aeolus tied the unfavorable winds so that Ulysses could reach home.

9. A reference to Odysseus' faithful wife who hardly dared believe that he was still alive after twenty years' absence.

10. The Cyclopes each had only one eye.

_____ Word Study _____

2. To undertake a difficult journey to some definite goal; to be in a lazy or lethargic state; prophecies which are not believed; anything

which is irresistably alluring; between a rock and a hard place or between the Devil and the deep blue sea.

3. A play on words. When Ulysses gives as his name a word which in the nominative case sounds like the Greek word for "no one."

_____ Questions for Review _____

1. They returned to Sparta after some [eight years of] wandering. [After a long life they were transported alive to the Islands of the Blest.] Agamemnon was murdered by Clytemnestra and Aegisthus.

2. As he wandered the world pursued by the Furies he happened to come to the land of the Tauri, where she had become a priestess of Artemis.

3. In the *Odyssey*: Ulysses also appears in the *Iliad.*

4. Twenty.

5. Seventy-two of his men were killed. Three of his crew had to be brought away by force because they had eaten lotus and lost all will to return home. Six of his men were eaten before he devised a way of escaping from Polyphemus' cave. He was given a bag in which all the winds except the one which would take him home were enclosed; on his second visit he was turned away. He lost all his ships but one. Some of his men were changed into swine; armed with the moly, he forced Circe to restore them, after which she became hospitable and entertained him for a year. He spoke with the shades of Tiresias, his mother, and some heroes of the Trojan War. He passed them successfully by having himself tied to the mast, while his crew's ears were stopped with wax. He avoided Charybdis and so lost six men to Scylla. His men, against his wishes, killed some of the cattle while he slept. He was kept a prisoner for eight years by Calypso. He was hospitably received and brought home one of their ships.

6. Totally destitute, disguised as a beggar.

7. A gang of young nobles who were his wife's suitors were eating him out of house and home.

8. His son Telemachus.

9. His old dog Argus.

10. Whoever strung Ulysses' bow and shot best with it was to have Penelope's hand in marriage.

11. He shot them dead.

12. He died on a pilgrimage [or was killed by his son Telegonus].

_____ Reading List _____

Poems and Plays

If your school produces musicals, perhaps you could induce them to put on *The Golden Apple*, a musical which transfers the events from the Judgment of Paris to the return of Ulysses to the State of Washington around the turn of the century. The events are cleverly adapted: the three ladies who run the social life of the town of Angel's Roost, Mrs. Juniper, the Mayor's wife, Miss Minerva Oliver, the schoolteacher, and Mrs. Lovey Mars, the matchmaker, fail to invite Mother Hare, an old witch-woman, to the Church Social. In revenge she presents a golden apple to be the prize for the Baked Goods Contest. Despairing of finding an unprejudiced native, they persuade a traveling salesman, a representative of Paris Notions, Inc., to be the judge. He is bribed by Lovey Mars, who introduces him to Helen, wife of Sheriff Menelaus. The expedition to bring her back from the big city, whose mayor is Hector, occupies the rest of the musical.

Prose

Because in the *Odyssey* Homer shows such a remarkable understanding of feminine psychology and such sympathy for his female characters and because he seems oddly ignorant of details of sailing and fighting which most men would know, Samuel Butler proposed, only half in jest, the theory that the *Odyssey* was composed by a woman. Robert Graves has turned this idea into an absorbing novel, *Homer's Daughter*, which, however unlikely its thesis, gives a convincing account of how an epic might have been put together out of personal experiences and scraps of folk tales, legend, and myth. It is well worth reading for anyone who has already read the *Odyssey*.

15   Adventures of Aeneas

From Troy to Carthage

Since the *Iliad* and the *Odyssey* are the earliest western works of literature we have, we can only speculate about the material that went into them. It is most likely that Homer made use of already existing myths, legends, and folk tales, and almost certain that he sang about gods and heroes already known to his audience; but we cannot *know*, since we have no earlier works to refer to. For all that we can prove, Homer may have invented every character and every incident in his two epics. Similarly, we cannot be sure of the composition of Homer's intended audience. We may imagine that he entertained nobles with songs of the doings of their ancestors, but again we cannot know. With Virgil and the *Aeneid* we are in quite a different situation. We know, insofar as any historical knowledge is reliable, who Virgil was, when he wrote, who were his audience, and at least one of his purposes in writing. We also know and can read quite a large number of earlier works which he had read and which he expected his readers to have read, as well.

One of Virgil's aims was to give to the growth and power of Rome a cosmic significance, grafting its history and its legends onto the existing mythology of the Hellenistic world. In doing so he was able to manipulate and make use of all the stories we have read so far. Treated analytically, the *Aeneid* can be made to seem a mere patchwork of allusions to earlier works. Of course it is much more than that. It is perhaps, from a literary point of view, the greatest poem ever written, but its extraordinary richness does, to some extent, depend on its ability to draw on other works and their significance.

This point may be illustrated in almost any passage of the work. When Aeneas, rescued from the Syrtes (the great sandbar from which Jason and the Argonauts were rescued), arrives on the shore of Africa, he meets his mother who has disguised herself as a young huntress. Aeneas, not recognizing her, greets her in words which echo the first words of Ulysses to Nausicaa when he was cast ashore in her land. As Venus leaves him, she drops her disguise too soon and Aeneas reproaches her for her elusiveness in the words of Ulysses to the shade of his mother in Hades, expressing his longing to embrace her.

When Aeneas reaches Carthage and Dido appears, she is introduced by a translation of the simile with which Homer introduces Nausicaa; a comparison of Nausicaa and her handmaidens, now of Dido and her court, to Diana surrounded by her nymphs. The effect is a complex one:

not only is the heroically capable and experienced widow Dido seen by us for a moment as a Nausicaa, an innocent, inexperienced, and vulnerable young girl, but Carthage becomes for Aeneas what the land of the Phaeacians was for Ulysses—a place where he may marry, settle down, and leave his toilsome journeys, yet a place which he will have to leave to continue his quest. Nausicaa in Homer is obsessed with the idea of marriage, whereas Dido has sworn never to marry again; the simile lets us see that Dido's determination not to marry may not be as unshakable as she supposes.

The primary comparison, to Diana, brings other connotations: Diana is a virgin goddess, dangerous for men to approach. Yet Aeneas has just come from an interview with Venus, the Goddess of Love, in a Diana-like disguise.

Allusions of this kind continue throughout the story of Aeneas' liaison with Dido and, when she learns that he is leaving her, her pleas and reproaches are borrowed from those of Ariadne, abandoned on Naxos, to Theseus (in Catullus 64) and those of Medea to Jason. All our feelings for those abandoned heroines are called up and we see Aeneas for the moment as an ungrateful wretch who has taken advantage of an innocent girl, forgetting that the situation is quite different.

Over and over again Aeneas is compared with Ulysses, to show us by his different reactions to the same situations how much more responsible, dutiful, and caring he is — attributes summed up in the epithet *pius* which replaces for him the *polytropos* ("wily") which Homer gives to Ulysses.

Juno's hatred of these Trojans sprang not only from the Judgment of Paris but also from her jealousy of the Trojan Ganymede and her knowledge that Aeneas' descendants would one day overthrow her own city of Carthage.

Aeneas' father Anchises was the son of Themis, a daughter of Ilus, the first King of Troy, and Capys, a son of Assaracus, the second. Aeneas himself was married to Creusa, a daughter of Priam and Hecuba. Hence his claim to kingship over the Trojans would have been a strong one even if he had not been Troy's only surviving hero.

Anchises had to be carried from Troy because he was lame. His lameness was a result (this story is not in the *Aeneid*) of his having boasted to his friends in his youth that his beauty had attracted the goddess of love herself. At a drinking-party one of his cronies had observed that the wife of a mutual friend was so beautiful that he would rather enjoy her than Venus herself. Anchises had replied, "Nonsense! Having tried both, I would much prefer Venus," and was immediately struck in the leg by a thunderbolt.

Aeneas' landing-place in Thrace, where he at first hoped to found his new city, happened to be at the burial-site of Polydorus (mentioned in the comments on the *Adventures of Ulysses*, Lesson 14). When he broke branches from a tree to burn his sacrifice, blood flowed from the break and the voice of Polydorus told the story of his murder. Aeneas was forced to leave a place so ill-omened for Trojans.

Calling at Delos to consult Apollo's oracle, Aeneas learned that he must settle in the ancient homeland of the Trojan race. Anchises, recalling that his great-great-great-great-grandfather Teucer had come from Crete, directed the Trojans there. Idomeneus having been banished and the island having been practically depopulated by the plague, there was room there for the new city. The Trojans had nearly completed the city and farming had begun, when the plague came again. The gods of Troy appeared to Aeneas and told him that Dardanus, Teucer's son-in-law, had come to Troy from Italy and that that was the place Apollo had meant. Anchises then recalled that Cassandra had prophesied that the future of Troy lay in Italy, but of course he hadn't believed her.

On leaving Crete the Trojans were driven by a storm to the Strophades, to which the sons of Boreas had driven the Harpies. Before the departure of the Trojans, the Harpy Celaeno delivered a prophecy confirming the fact that Italy was their destination, but warning them that before they could settle there they would be so hungry they would eat their tables. The prophecy was later harmlessly fulfilled when they had spread their food on large flat pieces of bread (like pita bread) and were eating them, and little Ascanius cried out, "Look! we are eating our tables."

They next stopped to rest at Actium (the place where later Augustus would win his decisive victory over Cleopatra) and held games there. After a long stay they moved on to Chaonia where they found to their delight that the King and Queen were fellow-Trojans, Helenus and Andromache, who had been left in charge by the death of Neoptolemus. They were received hospitably and loaded with gifts. Before they left, the seer Helenus gave them further instructions. They were not to head for the nearby eastern coast of Italy, since the cities there were all in the hands of Greeks (Idomeneus and Philoctetes among them), but were to go to its western shore. To do this they would have to go around Sicily, to avoid Scylla and Charybdis at the Straits of Messina. Helenus also told Aeneas that for further information he would have to consult the Sibyl at Cumae.

Having narrowly escaped Charybdis by hard rowing, the Trojans landed next on the eastern shore of Sicily, near Mt. Etna; this is where they picked up Achaemenides, the sailor left behind by Ulysses.

Dido was a historical figure, a princess of Tyre in Phoenicia. Her real name was Eliza (which the Romans wrote as *Elissa*, because the original Latin alphabet had no z); *Dido*, a Phoenician word meaning "wanderer," was a nickname given her by her followers after she had succeeded in founding Carthage. Her ancestry is of interest since it connects her with several well-known Old Testament figures.

The legitimate King of Tyre, a descendant of Solomon's friend and partner King Hiram, was deposed and put to death in 917 B.C. by Ethbaal, a priest of Astarte. Ethbaal had a son and a daughter, Balezor and Jezebel. It was this Jezebel who was married to King Ahab of Israel and led him into Baal-worship, so that he "did more to provoke the Lord God of Israel to anger than all the kings that were before him." Balezor succeeded his father in 885 and died himself in 877, leaving the kingship to his son Mutton. Mutton had two children, Eliza and Pumiyathon (whom the Greeks and Romans called Pygmalion); he married Eliza to her uncle, his younger brother Sicharbaal (called Sychaeus by Virgil), a priest of Melkart. When Mutton died in 853 he left the realm to Pumiyathon and Eliza. However, when he was sixteen, Pumiyathon led a rebellion, seized the throne for himself, and put Sicharbaal to death. Eliza, accompanied by the loyalist party, took the treasures of Tyre and fled to Africa where she founded Carthage (*Kart-Hadasht*, "New City"). So Dido was a great-niece of Jezebel.

Since the end of the Trojan War is traditionally dated at around 1200 B.C., the dates do not fit in very well, but the Romans had a great deal of difficulty in harmonizing their chronology with that of Greek tradition and history. The story that Aeneas had stopped at Carthage on his way to Italy became current at Rome during the Punic Wars as a kind of historical justification for the enmity between Rome and Carthage.

After leaving Carthage, the Trojans stopped in Sicily to celebrate the funeral games of Anchises. Their host was Acestes, the son of Segesta, a Trojan woman whom her father had sent to Sicily to escape the war, and the river-god Crimisus. Here was celebrated, among other athletic events, the famous Game of Troy (mentioned in the comments on *Europa and her Kin* in Lesson 3), led by Ascanius. During the games some of the women, tired of wandering and happy to find a welcoming land with a Trojan king, set fire to the ships. With the help of the gods the fire was extinguished, but Aeneas decided to leave behind all the fainthearted; for them he laid out a city in Sicily.

In the Underworld

The Cumaean Sibyl, like the Pythia at Delphi, was the mouthpiece of an oracle of Apollo. Her method of keeping her oracles ambiguous was to spread leaves on the floor of her chamber and write her response on them. When the door was opened the leaves were scattered by the draft and the questioner had to reassemble them as best he could. The Sibyl did, however, collect some of her prophecies into books and sold them to Tarquin the Proud, Rome's seventh and last King. These books were consulted only at the command of the Senate in times of great danger, as when the cults of Asclepius and of Demeter, Kore, and Dionysus were imported into Rome.

Because in early Christian times forged versions of the Sibylline Books were circulated which contained prophecies of the birth of Christ, the Middle Ages included the Cumaean Sibyl, or occasionally all the Sibyls, among the Prophets and they appear sometimes among the decorations of churches. The convention was continued into the Renaissance; this is the reason for their appearance on the ceiling of Michelangelo's Sistine Chapel.

The Cumaean Sibyl, whose name was Herophile, was supposed to be immortal, but (like Tithonus) not eternally youthful. As she grew older and more withered she retired to a cave beneath the temple of Apollo. In historical times charlatans used to exhibit a tiny dried-up creature in a bottle which they claimed to be the Sibyl, and would sell oracles which they produced by ventriloquism.

The Grotto of the Sibyl at Cumae is an impressive gallery cut in the living rock, and well worth a visit from anyone who happens to be in the neighborhood of Naples.

In Italy

Evander the Arcadian, a son of Mercury and the river-nymph Themis (whom the Romans called Carmenta), had brought a colony from Arcadia to Italy, where he settled on the Palatine Hill (so called, the Romans supposed, from the name of his son Pallas). Evander was old by the time Aeneas met him, having been already settled on the Palatine at the time of Hercules' slaying of Cacus. It was Evander who instituted the worship of Hercules at the site of Rome.

The ships of Aeneas had been built of pines sacred to Cybele, who had obtained from Jupiter permission to protect them from destruction. When Turnus burst into the Trojan camp and attempted to fire the ships, they were metamorphosed into sea-nymphs.

In their search for allies the Latins sent an embassy to Aeneas' old enemy Diomedes, in his city of Arpi; but he refused to renew the Trojan War in Italy and, knowing Aeneas' might, advised the Latins to make peace.

Romulus and Remus

Conflicting legends that Rome had been founded by Aeneas, the son of Venus, and by Romulus, the son of Mars, were harmonized by making Romulus a descendant of Aeneas. As the Romans gradually became more aware of the span of time between the Trojan War and the founding of Rome in 753 B.C. (a traditional date borne out by archaeological investigations) they kept adding to the list of Kings of Alba Longa, until in Livy the genealogy runs: Ascanius, Silvius, Aeneas Silvius, Latinus Silvius, Alba, Atys, Capys, Capetus, Tiberinus, Agrippa, Romulus Silvius, Aventinus, Proca, Numitor. Numitor was driven from his throne by his younger brother Amulius, who put Numitor's sons to death and made his daughter, Rhea Silvia, a Vestal Virgin so that she could have no offspring. She nevertheless became by Mars the mother of Romulus and Remus. When they were grown they killed Amulius and restored their grandfather to his throne. They then went off to found Rome.

PRACTICAL APPLICATIONS

_____ References to Mythology in Literature _____

1. Sibyls were oracular priestesses of Apollo.

2. Before Aeneas could enter the Lower World he had to find the Golden Bough.

3. Shores near Lavinium; the reference is specifically to the opening line of the *Aeneid*: "Arms and the man I sing, the first who came, / Compelled by Fate, an exile out of Troy, / To Italy and the Lavinian Shores. . ."

4. Ascanius was Aeneas' son by Priam's daughter Creusa; the reference is to the time when Venus, wishing to make Dido love Aeneas, .disguised Cupid as Ascanius and sent him to Dido, while she herself kept the true Ascanius asleep on her lap.

5. Dido, abandoned by Aeneas, stood on the the shore and tried to call him back.

_____ Word Study _____

1. From the ambiguous replies of the Sibyls, oracular priestesses of Apollo. From the Harpies, foul bird-women who snatched the food from people's tables.

3. Anna (though most people called by this name trace it back to St. Anna, the legendary mother of the Virgin Mary; it is, however, the same name, being a variant of the Hebrew/Phoenician *Hannah*), Sibyl, Lavinia, Camilla, Iris, Diana, and Julius.

4. Cape Palinurus and Lavinia. The Romans supposed that it was from

Romulus, but this is actually etymologically impossible: Romulus must have been named from Rome. To caper, to perform antics.

_____ Questions for Review _____

1. A prince of Troy, son of Anchises and Venus.

2. Leading his son by the hand and carrying his father, he gathered the survivors together and took ship for Thrace.

3. Italy.

4. The Harpies snatched away the food from their tables. They rescued one of Ulysses' men whom he had left behind.

5. By not passing through the Straits of Messina.

6. Juno.

7. She persuaded Aeolus to stir up a storm which ran the Trojans aground on the Syrtes.

8. By dislodging the ships.

9. In Africa, near Carthage.

10. [Elissa, known as] Dido.

11. Yes.

12. She cursed him and committed suicide.

13. The death of Palinurus.

14. The Cumaean Sibyl.

15. The Lower World.

16. The Furies, Death, Hunger, Fear, hydras, chimeras, Cerberus, Dido, Trojans and Greeks from the war, Palinurus, Ixion, Tantalus, Orpheus, and Anchises.

17. The great men of Rome.

18. The shore near Lavinium. The daughter of King Latinus.

19. Turnus. The war between the Trojans and the Latins.

20. A virgin huntress, a favorite of Diana.

21. Arcadians who had settled at the site of Rome.

22. Their hated deposed king, Mezentius, had taken refuge with Turnus.

23. They were killed by the Latins as they tried to carry a message to Aeneas.

24. With a javelin, by Aruns.

25. Aeneas.

26. Romulus and Remus who left Alba Longa to start a new city for their followers.

27. Mars.

28. They were exposed but rescued by a she-wolf and brought up by a shepherd and his wife.

29. Rome.

30. Over the naming of the city.

_____ Reading List _____

Virgil's contemporary, the historian Livy, reports in Book I of his *History* some of the same events as Virgil describes in the *Aeneid*. It is interesting to compare these two works which are so different in their attitude. It is also interesting to see in Book I of the *History* how myth merges gradually into legend and legend into history. Livy does not really feel that the gods intervene directly in human affairs, so his approach is euhemeristic to the point of de-bunking: even his myths and legends are treated historically. It is in this book that famous figures like Mucius Scaevola and Horatius (at the bridge) may be found.

16   Divinities of Rome

Janus and Saturn

The Greeks on the whole tended to think that other nations' gods were not the same as their own gods, and they never made the wholesale identification of foreign gods with their own that the Romans did. The Romans naively assumed that all the world worshipped the same gods and, when they met a foreign god, tried from his attributes to discover who he really was and what his Latin name would be. The identifications were often based on superficial resemblances. The near-eastern Astarte, for example, was called variously Diana, Juno, and Venus, depending on the circumstances under which the Romans ran across her. Only when they found no resemblance at all to one of their own gods would a god be admitted under his own name (like Apollo). Since (if we include all the *numina* which had names) the Romans had hundreds, perhaps thousands of gods, they could not all be absorbed by their Greek counterparts. Hence there are some gods left over who are strictly Roman. These gods seldom have much mythology or personality.

Like other strictly Roman gods, Janus has little mythology. We are forced to deduce the history of his divinity from his place in ritual and prayer. It is probable that he was originally the *numen* of the doorway, since his name appears as a common noun meaning "the arch of a gate." The earliest references to Janus refer not to a god, but to a building, the Janus in the Forum at Rome.

In Italy, where most of the rivers are seasonal torrents, there are many fords. These have been marked from antiquity to the present by two pairs of poles, one pair on each side of the stream, each pair joined at the top by a horizontal piece of wood. Markers of the same kind are used to show the location also of simple footbridges.

The original site of Rome, the Palatine Hill, was no doubt chosen because it was almost surrounded by water. A small stream called Cloaca flowed into the Tiber to the north and west of the hill. Another, the Consus, flowed along its east and south sides from a lake where the Colosseum now stands, emptying into the Tiber near the mouth of the Cloaca.

Although these small streams would have slowed down an enemy attack, their real importance in the fortification of Rome was magical. Since magic powers cannot cross running water, the streams kept invaders from bringing their magic into the city. However, they would also have kept the Romans from bringing theirs to the public meetings of the Forum or to the religious services of the Cattle-Market, if the High Priest, called from this function the "Bridge-Builder" (*pontifex*, from which our word "pontiff" is derived), had not made magical crossings. A footbridge marked at each end by an arch gave access from the Palatine Hill to the Forum, a market- and meeting-place; another gave access to the riverside cattle-market and the Great Altar of Hercules. These bridges were the *Jani*. When the two streams were later covered over, the two Januses remained. Since the streams were now (except in magical terms) crossable at any point, these sets of arches connected by walls, now built in masonry for permanence, had only a magical/religious significance. They were still the route by which the priests could bring their magic into and out of the city. The magic of the Jani was kept in by gates at each end. In time of war these were opened to let the magic escape so that no enemy could bring his power in.

The *numen* of these magical bridges naturally became the god of gates, then of doorways, then of any beginnings: of the first day of the year and each month, of springs, and of the dawn. Because he was invoked at the beginning of prayers to the gods, he began to be thought of as a very great god, called the Good Creator, the God of Gods, and the Oldest of the Gods. He is sometimes called a god of the sky, like Uranus, the oldest of the Greek gods. His title *Consivius* may indicate some connection with Consus, as may the title *Consiva* given to Saturn's wife Ops. His other name, "Father Matutinus," suggests also some connection with Mother Matuta, a goddess of the maturation of children to adolescence.

Besides the cakes and coins, another common New Year's gift was a terra-cotta lamp on which in low relief was depicted the winged goddess of Victory surrounded by coins and sweetmeats and holding a shield on which she has written, "A happy and prosperous New Year to you."

Like many Roman gods, Janus was thought of as having lived on earth, in his case on the Janiculum, a hill just outside Rome. Similarly, Saturn lived on the Capitoline Hill in the heart of Rome.

When the Cloaca and the Consus were enclosed, their *numina* were repaid by being given areas which were sacred to them: that of Consus was an underground altar on the central division of the great racetrack built in his valley, where he was worshipped as "Neptune of the Horses." Cloaca's was a small round enclosure in the Forum, where she was honored as Venus ("Charm") of Cloaca, *Venus Cloacina*. Since this underground stream became the chief sewer of Rome, the word *cloaca* came to mean "sewer," and *Venus Cloacina* "Venus of the Sewer," a strange combination. Cloaca may also have been a goddess of fertility, since near her mouth was built the temple of Fortuna Virilis ("Men's Fertility"), whose holy day, April 1, was the same as that of Venus Verticordia ("Softener of Hearts"). The dedication day of the temple of Fortuna Virilis was the same as that of the nearby temple of Mother Matuta, a goddess who was worshipped by women who had been married only once. Since they prayed to her for the health of their nieces and nephews she was identified with Leucothea, who had been Ino, Dionysus' aunt who nursed him as a baby.

The other topographical feature which made the Palatine an ideal site for the first city of Rome was the landing-place on the Tiber, the low, shelving bank where the Cloaca and Consus had their mouths, in a reach sheltered by the Tiber Island. The *numen* of this landing was Portunus, who also had his temple near those of Fortuna and Matuta. He was later identified with Palaemon, who had been Ino's son Melicertes.

The Roman gods' lack of personality caused them to merge and multiply in a way very uncharacteristic of the Greek gods. Cloaca and Venus were two goddesses, yet they were one and the same; Consus and Neptune were separate, yet one. Diana, when she was addressed as the goddess of childbirth, was called Lucina; but Lucina was also Juno, so that Diana could be addressed as Juno Lucina. Juno was one goddess, the wife and sister of Jupiter, yet every woman had a Juno of her own, a kind of guardian angel. Aeneas was worshipped as Jupiter. Quirinus was Mars, but Romulus, the son of Mars, was Quirinus. Cybele and Rhea were sometimes called Ops; Ops and Cybele are each the Good Goddess, but the Good Goddess is Maia, who is also called Fauna.

Many more of these early, strictly Roman gods could be mentioned, but these are enough to give some idea of how they differ from the gods of the Greeks.

Saturn may not, in fact, have been originally a Roman god. Historians of religion can distinguish between the native gods and those imported from Greece by the nature of their worship, the simplest distinction being that a priest sacrificing to a Roman god covered his head with a fold of his toga (to keep him from hearing any ill-omened sounds), while to the imported Greek gods he sacrificed bareheaded. Saturn was one of those to whom sacrifice was offered in the Greek manner; hence it may be that the myth of his having been welcomed to Italy by Janus may echo some early importation of a Greek god. His character and functions differ so from those of Cronus, however, that it is hard to see why that particular identification was made.

The gifts that were exchanged during the Saturnalia included candles and little dolls.

Lesser Roman Deities

Carmenta, the mother of Evander, was sometimes included among the Camenae; she was a goddess of childbirth and prophecy. In the typical but confusing Roman way, she is at the same time two different goddesses;

Prorsa, goddess of foretelling the future and of normal births, and Post-vorta, goddess of revealing the past and of breech births.

By a reversal of the usual process, the Greek goddess Tyche borrowed her divinity and her attributes from Fortuna. Tyche was a popular patron goddess of cities in Hellenistic times. As such, in addition to her other attributes, she wears a crown made to look like the walls of a city, the "mural crown." In turn, Roman city goddesses borrowed back from Tyche some of her attributes: for example, the Venus of Pompeii is shown with the mural crown and steering oar.

Bellona was later identified with the Greek minor goddess Enyo, a companion of Ares. Oddly, when at the beginning of the Ist Century B.C. the goddess Ma (another name for Cybele, the Great Mother, who was herself identified with Rhea and Ops) was imported from Cappadocia, she was called Bellona by the Romans.

Terminus inhabited every duly consecrated boundary-stone, but his chief abode was a stone on the Capitoline Hill in Rome. When Tarquin the Proud built the first temple to Jupiter Capitolinus there, Terminus (according to the official soothsayers) refused to move. Therefore a hole had to be left in the roof above his stone, since Terminus was always worshipped in the open air.

Silvanus is another deity who may appear as a number of individual gods. In the singular he is sometimes identified with Pan (and he is the causer of panic fear); in the plural with the Satyrs. Since *silvanus* is an adjective rather than a name, some scholars believe him to have been an aspect of Faunus, "the silvan Faunus." He is usually shown as a jolly old man and as such is sometimes identified with Silenus.

Faunus was more usually identified with Pan; he did not cause panic fear but, under the name of Fatuus ("speaker") he was the source of the strange unidentifiable sounds heard in the woods. He may have been the same as Incubo, who was a mischievous goblin, the god of nightmares. Anyone who could succeed in stealing Incubo's cap could force him to reveal where treasure was buried; in this he resembled a leprechaun. The younger fauns who accompanied Faunus are like the Panisci ("little Pans") who in later art and literature accompany Pan.

Lupercus was sometimes identified with Faunus and hence with Pan; Luperca was sometimes called Fauna or Fatua.

Pomona actually has a little myth, though it may have been invented by Ovid. The god Vertumnus loved her but she was interested only in working in her orchards and vineyards. To be near her, Vertumnus adopted many disguises. Finally, in the guise of an old woman, he pointed out to her that the grapevine would not bear fruit if it were not supported on a tree, and suggested that she was like such a grapevine. Convinced by this analogy taken from her own field of interest, she gave in and married Vertumnus when he next came wooing in his own shape.

Flora was an important goddess in Italy though not especially so in Rome: she was the patron goddess of Pompeii before Venus. During her festival people wore bright clothes and were entertained by grossly indecent dramatic performances.

Hymen is a Greek name, but to the Greeks Hymen was not a god, but merely a hero; it was the Romans who made him a god. They sometimes called him Talassio.

If current interpretations of paintings and sculptures found in the household shrines excavated at various Roman sites are correct, each household had one or two Lares and as many Penates as it chose. The Lares are depicted as young men in girt-up tunics and high boots, dancing while they pour wine (or some liquid) from drinking-horns into little pails. Alternatively they may be shown as large serpents, sometimes with crests or with crests and beards. In this form a Lar is identified as *genius loci*, the guardian spirit of a place. In houses in Italy there are always two of them; outside Italy there is only one. The reason for this is that when Aeneas fled Troy he was allowed by a special dispensation of the gods to bring the Lar of Troy with him. Ordinarily the Lar remained attached to the place, so that when one moved the Lar was left behind. The Penates, however, went along with the family. Hence every household in Italy had two Lares, the Lar of the particular place and the Lar of Troy. Abroad there was only the Lar of the place.

In wall paintings the Lares are often accompanied by the *genius* or guardian spirit of the head of the household, shown as a man wearing the toga and pouring an offering from an offering-bowl. Every man had a Genius, just as every woman had a Juno.

The Penates were whatever gods the family might select. For example, a Pompeian might choose the Venus of Pompeii, Minerva (if he was part of the great cloth industry there), Mercury (if he hoped to make money), and Hercules (if he belonged to the Juventus). Apparently unlikely intruders sometimes appear amongst the Penates, the gods of Egypt or the Near East, Perseus, and (in the chapel of Alexander Severus) Moses and Jesus.

Since the Romans supposed that nearly every object and action had its own *numen*, there was a great number of minor divinities. The names of a few, taken from those who watched over the family, will give some idea of the minuteness of the subdivisions of divine functions. Domiduca was the goddess of the movement of a bride from her father's to her husband's house. Unxia was the goddess of smearing perfumed olive oil on the doorposts of the groom's house before the arrival of the bride. Cinxia was in charge of untying the bride's belt. Pronuba brought the bride to the marriage ceremony and turned her over to Juga, who presided over the ceremony. After Juno and Carmenta and the other Camenae had presided over the birth of a baby, Ossipaga strengthened its bones and

Carna put flesh on them. When it was weaned, Potina helped it to learn to drink, then Educa taught it to eat. Cuba helped it in the transition from sleeping in a cradle to sleeping in a bed. Levana aided it to sit upright and Statanus to stand up. Adeona was there when it began to walk to its parents, and Abeona assisted it to walk away from them. Fabulinus helped it to learn to talk. These are only a few of the gods involved in family life alone; it is to be remembered that, with the exception of Juno and the Camenae, none of these gods had any other functions. It is easy to see why the Romans had practically no mythology and very little theogony of their own.

PRACTICAL APPLICATIONS

_____ Specific Literary References _____

1. Fauns and satyrs are minor woodland deities of the Romans and Greeks, respectively.

2. Flora is used by paronomasia for blossoming nature.

3. The spirits of the dead or of a dead person.

4. The Lares are spirits of a place, in this case Etruria; the towers of Mars are the fortifications of Rome, the city founded by Mars' son Romulus.

5. The god of weddings.

6. Silvanus, god of wild uncultivated nature.

7. Saturn's temple was on the slopes of the Capitoline Hill, the nucleus of Rome.

8. The woodland god of animals and hence of shepherds.

9. Saturn was identified with the grim god Cronus.

10. Merry festivities, from the Romans' winter festival of Saturn.

11. The Roman two-faced god of gateways and beginning, oldest of the gods.

12. The Roman goddess of war.

13. The god of weddings.

14. The goddess of fruits.

15. The god of the uncultivated countryside.

_____ Word Study _____

1. From *Saturnalia*, the merry Roman feast of Saturn. From the golden age when *Saturn* ruled at Rome. From *Janus*, god of beginnings. From *terminus*, the Latin for "boundary-stone," which also became the name of the god of boundaries. From *silva*, the Latin word for "woods," which also gave the god Silvanus his name. From *Hymen*, the god of weddings. From the Latin word *flos, floris*, from which Flora derives her name. From *janus*, a Latin word for a doorway, which was also the name of the god of doorways. From the Latin *ops*, "richness, luxuriance," also the name of Saturn's wife. From the Latin *pomum*, "fruit," from which Pomona derives her name.

2. *Jovial. mercurial. martial* (when used to describe someone's character), and *saturnine* all refer to the astrological influence at the time of one's birth. The nature of the influence is connected with the character of the god for whom each is named. The influence of Saturn has not much to do with the pleasant god of the Romans, but with Cronus, his grim and melancholy Greek counterpart. In its more usual application *martial* means "like Mars, the god of war." *March*, the month of the vernal equinox, was named for Mars in his aspect as god of the sprouting grain. *Volcanoes* were thought to be Vulcan's workshops (*Volcano* is the Italian for "Vulcan"). Vulcan's name was frequently used by paronomasia for "fire;" vulcanization involves applying heat to rubber. The month of *June*, for unknown reasons, was named for Juno. The Romans often used *Ceres* to mean "grain;" hence *cereal* means "having to do with grain." *Vestal* can mean "belonging to Vesta," but it more often refers to the Vestal Virgins, the pagan convent of nuns who looked after Vesta's rites. The seven days of the Roman religious week were named after the seven "planets:" the Sun, the Moon, Mars, Mercury, Jupiter, Venus, and Saturn. *Saturday* is Saturn's day. English preserves the old naming of Saturday and Sunday, which in most of the Romance languages are called "the Sabbath" and "the Lord's Day." They, however, keep the names of the Roman gods for Tuesday through Friday, which in English have the names of Norse gods. Applied strictly, *Bacchic* means "of Bacchus" or "of the worship of Bacchus;" more loosely it refers to unbridled revelry, especially if drinking is involved. *Plutocrat* is derived from the Greek words for "riches" and "power;" the first of these is the source of Hades' euphemistic nickname Pluto, "he who is growing rich." "*Panic* fear" is the sudden inexplicable alarm which stampedes a herd or routs an army in

battle; it is associated with Pan, the god of herds. *Satire* is derived from the Latin *satura*, "a mixed dish," but it has been influenced in its meaning and spelling by an early folk-etymology which connected it with the mischievous Satyrs. *Music* (like *mosaic*) was originally an adjective meaning "of the Muses;" but since seven of the Muses preside over different kinds of music, this is what the Greeks and Romans meant by what they called "the music art," later shortened to just "music." A *Museum* was originally a temple of the Muses. *Aurora* was the goddess of the dawn. *Chronology* is from the Greek word for "time," later personified as the god Chronus.

4. Zeus/Jupiter (Jove), Ares/Mars, Artemis/Diana, Pallas Athena/Minerva, Hermes/Mercury, Demeter/Ceres, Herakles/Hercules.

5. She is the inspiration of some man or the power behind some throne. The vegetable and animal denizens of a region.

_____ Questions for Review _____

1. Not originally, though many were later identified with and assimilated to them.

2. They admired their mythology.

3. The two-faced god of gateways and beginnings. The kindly god of sowing.

4. Peace and prosperity.

5. The holidays of the feast of Saturn.

6. Ops.

7. Egeria.

8. The goddess of luck. The goddess of war. The god of the boundary-stone. A god of uncultivated land.

9. Mischievous young divinities with some some goat characteristics who roamed the woodlands.

10. Lupercus and Luperca.

11. Pomona.

12. Hymen.

13. The gods of the household. The spirits of the dead.

14. The Tiber; because they were afraid that if they did not he would flood the city.

17 Myths in Ancient Literature

Homer, Hesiod, and Pindar

Homer and Hesiod both lived during the Greek dark ages, a period which is as dark to us as it was to the ancients. Their mythology provided for them a continuous account of their history and ancestry (however distorted by their religious beliefs) from the beginning of the Bronze Age to the end of the Heroic Age, which closes with the Homecomings, the return of the kings from the Trojan War. Archaeology does much the same for us; but neither tradition nor excavation has much to tell us about the time which intervened between the xɪɪth and the vɪɪɪth Centuries B.C. Things had clearly happened during this four-hundred-year lowering of the curtain: cities which were important places had disappeared or dwindled to villages, while other powerful cities had appeared or grown from insignificant places; the Peloponnesus, which had been inhabited by Ionian Greeks, was now full of Dorians. We know also, as the ancients did not, that the knowledge of writing had apparently been lost and rediscovered. At the time of the Trojan War the Greeks were using a syllabary borrowed from the Cretans; when they re-emerged into the light of history they had the Phoenician-derived alphabet which they are still using today.

The Greeks themselves attempted to fill the gap by a kind of extrapolation from both ends, hypothesizing, for example, the Return of the Heraclidae, in which the dispossessed descendants of Hercules, assisted by Dorians from the north, invaded the Peloponnesus to reclaim their ancestral lands. We call this incursion the Dorian Invasion, but we have little more evidence to go on than the ancients had.

Homer's lifetime is to be dated somewhere in this time. It has been placed, in both ancient and modern times, anywhere from 1200 to 700 B.C. Some scholars have narrowed this time span to the vɪɪɪth Century; but this dating depends on passages in the epics which may have been interpolations. All we can say for certain is that Homer lived after the Trojan War and before other writers began citing his works.

Homer is himself an almost mythical figure. Like the heroes of myth, he was worshipped after his death on the island of Ios where he was supposed to have died. The tradition that he died of chagrin at his inability to solve the riddle about the fleas is typical of the stories which attached themselves to his name, the point being that the riddle was so difficult that even the great Homer could not have answered it. He becomes in such stories an almost allegorical figure. Yet, in spite of all the legends attached to his name, the ancients never doubted that there had been such a person nor that he had composed at least one of the two great epics ascribed to him. (There were a few ancient scholars who thought that the *Odyssey* was by someone else.) It remained for modern times to cast doubt on his existence: at the end of the xviiith Century a German scholar put forward the theory that the *Iliad* and the *Odyssey* were simply collections of old songs about the Trojan War first assembled and written down in the vith Century B.C. He did not believe that any poet could have composed and remembered poems of such length and complexity without the aid of writing. Even though his theory was contradicted by the obvious unity and the artful structure of each epic, many followed him in his belief right up into our century. Now it has been shown that in many cultures (modern Greece among them) illiterate singers and storytellers are able to recite from memory pieces even longer than the two epics. Today a vast majority of scholars believes that Homer existed and was one person, explaining differences between the *Iliad* and the *Odyssey* by the difference of subject matter and by the assumption that Homer composed the *Iliad* in his youth and the *Odyssey* much later. One can understand the schoolboy who answered what has been called the "Homeric Question" with "Homer was. not written by Homer but somebody else of that name."

Homer tells us nothing about himself in his poetry; Hesiod, on the other hand, includes quite a lot of autobiographical material in the *Works and Days* and some even in the *Theogony*. He had emigrated with his father and his brother Perses from Cyme in Aeolia to Ascra near Mt. Helicon in Boeotia. When the father died Perses took more than his rightful share of the estate, then later sued Hesiod to obtain even more. We do not hear from him how this lawsuit turned out but there are legends, mutually contradictory, which give accounts of it and of the rest of his life.

Hesiod's dates are uncertain: guesses range from the time of Homer (whenever that was) down to a century later, with most scholars nowadays suggesting the time of the First Olympiad, 776 B.C.

Pindar is a fully historical figure: we know his dates (518-438), his family and parentage, and his travels throughout the Greek world, including Sicily. Four of the seventeen books he wrote have survived. In them are the victory hymns, some to be sung at the site of the victory, but most to be performed in the winner's home town. He tends to refine the myths he uses, giving them a moral character and rejecting such primitive elements as the story that Demeter ate Pelops' shoulder.

Virgil

Strangely enough, Virgil does not show us the growth of Roman imperial power as Utopian or even desirable, but rather as inevitable. He manages to make it clear that all history, both human and divine, has been moving unswervingly toward this end. Although the narrative ends with the death of Turnus, he has shown us the true end — or rather the endlessness — of his story in the prophecies of Anchises to Aeneas in the Lower World. His ending is not really a happy one; he feels too much regret for the innocent lives which must be ruined or lost: Dido's, Euryalus', Turnus', etc. It is perhaps worth pointing out that Juno's curse upon Aeneas, the fulfillment of which she fears will be denied her by the Fates, actually comes true in every clause: he is required to leave behind or to see the death of everyone whom he loves, except Ascanius. In return he is not even to found the New Troy of which he has dreamt but must leave it for his descendants.

Since so many works of earlier Latin writers have been lost, we cannot be sure just how much of the mythology of the *Aeneid* was Virgil's own invention. He may, for example, have been the first to make Dido and Aeneas fall in love. He was almost certainly the first to grant a higher place in the pantheon to some of the local *numina* of Rome. For example, Portunus, the divinity of the river-landing at Rome, appears off the coast of Sicily as an important god of the sea.

In spite of his later date and known position in history, Virgil became the object of even more mythologizing than did Homer. In the Fourth Eclogue he prophesied the coming birth of a child which would be accompanied by the appearance of the Virgin (meaning Themis) and the restoration of the Age of Saturn, the Golden Age. Nature would be tamed, the sheep would not fear the lion, the serpent would lose his poison. The boy who was to be born was to rule a world at peace, with sorrow and hardships banished. It is no wonder that the Middle Ages saw this Eclogue as an undoubted prophecy of the birth of Jesus, whom they saw likewise to have been called the Prince of Peace in Old Testament prophecies.

This extraordinary coincidence led to the creation of the mytholo-gized Virgil — or rather of two different Virgils. In one set of legends he is a great prophet and takes his place in art and literature alongside Isaiah and the rest of the Prophets. Typical of this view is the story that St. Paul, on his arrival in Italy, paid a visit to the tomb of Virgil. He found his body perfectly preserved, sitting at a writing-table with pen in hand, a lighted lamp nearby. As Paul entered, the body and all the furniture crumbled to dust. Paul's arrival had signalled the moment which the prophet-poet had awaited.

The other tradition made Virgil acquire his foreknowledge of the birth of Jesus by magic. He was the great magician who had played Merlin to Augustus' Arthur. The great buildings whose ruins could still be seen at Rome had all been built by him. The niches of the Pantheon had contained statues representing all the foreign nations. When war threat-ened from any of them, the statue of an archer in the center would turn and aim an arrow at the nation from which danger was to come. He set two gigantic statues up on the walls of the city and they everlastingly played a game of catch with a great stone ball for the entertainment of the Romans. He also set up a great stone face with an open mouth as a kind of lie detector: anyone who told a lie while holding his hand in its mouth would have his hand bitten off. This great carving (actually an ancient drain-cover) can still be seen in Rome: it is called the "Mouth of Truth" and some believe it is still working.

This set of legends about the poet is responsible for the changing of his name from *Vergilius* to *Virgilius*, since a *virga* is a magic wand. The legends which made him a Prophet also welcomed the change, since he had prophesied the coming of a *Virgin* (*Virgo*).

Ovid

One of the problems which Augustus faced when the Civil Wars finally set him on the throne was that of reform. Late Republican society had been immoral and frivolous, its politics corrupt, its culture elegant but over-luxurious, its intellectual life brilliant but cynical, its religious thought shallow and agnostic. Augustus wished to restore the values of an older Rome: respect for the old ways, for the gods, for the state, and for the family. In this Virgil helped him: the *Georgics*, while hardly the kind of handbook of farming which a practical farmer would carry about with him, inspired a new respect for the life of the country; the *Aeneid* revived the old Roman virtues and offered a view of the gods which could be accepted by the intellectuals of his day. Virgil's gods may not have inspired belief but they did inspire reverence. They were somewhat remote and superhuman in their natures. Even Juno's animosity against Aeneas is not petty but on the grand scale: she is concerned with the destiny of nations more than with the fate of this one man.

Ovid's immensely popular writings (he is quoted, for example, more than all other authors put together in the graffiti of Pompeii) must have damaged Augustus' plans for reform at least as much as Virgil's helped them. His gods and heroes, in both the *Metamorphoses* and the *Fasti* — and certainly in the *Epistolae* — are not reverend or even respectable: they are simply the Beautiful People of Ovid's own day in divine or heroic disguises. Examples could be multiplied indefinitely from every story he tells. Apollo, in pursuit of Daphne, fears that all this running will tire the lady and offers to run a little more slowly if she would like to slow her pace. The nymphs, in mourning for the dead Orpheus, stop employing their hairdressers and wear black borders on their dresses. Everything is humanized and trivialized, but always in the most elegant way.

Ovid's story-telling ability is superb: the very way in which he intertwines his stories, introducing every myth in some ingenious way, is masterly. It is no wonder that Augustus had to banish him.

His work, like Virgil's, connects Roman history with Greek mythology: his last metamorphosis is the apotheosis of Julius Caesar. But his tongue-in-cheek attitude keeps his work from becoming a hymn to Rome's greatness; rather it lowers the dignity of the empire. He begins his work by addressing Augustus as the human equivalent of Jupiter, then proceeds to tell a number of stories of Jupiter's extramarital exploits.

Ovid himself says that his banishment was brought about by "a book and a mistake." It is easy to see why the book made it necessary for Augustus to get rid of him.

We should not leave the brief account of Roman sources of myth without mentioning Nero's tutor, the philosopher Seneca, who in his tragedies introduced many references to mythology (especially to the lesser-known myths) which are our only evidence for some of the incidents.

PRACTICAL APPLICATIONS

_____ References to These Authors in Literature _____

1. Pindar was the vith-Century Greek author of Victory Odes, from which we derive our knowledge of many myths.

2. Homer was Greece's greatest epic poet; Virgil was Rome's.

3. Homer was the author of the *Iliad* and the *Odyssey*; these were his "domain."

4. The *Odyssey*, telling of the return of Odysseus from Troy, was Homer's second work.

5. In the *Aeneid* Virgil tells of the fall of Troy (Ilion) and the suicide of Queen Dido.

6. A reference to the Trojan Horse, a stratagem devised by Ulysses.

_____ Word Study _____

1. *Music* was originally an adjective meaning "of the Muses;" because seven of the nine were concerned with music. The term "music art," later shortened to "music," came to mean what it does today.

2. Yes, they all contain the root of the Latin verb *spiro*, "I breathe."

3. *Homeric* = "superhuman, heroic," like the battles of the heroes in the *Iliad*. *Pindar's* odes, actually very well organized, appear at first to introduce irrelevancies and to leap from topic to topic, until the threads are all carefully gathered in at the end. Smoothness is characteristic of *Virgil*; "happy," in this context, refers to his ability to make his somewhat artificial, carefully-thought-out diction seem natural.

4. "I fear the Greeks, even bearing gifts," "a sop to Cerberus," "the easy descent to the Underworld," "if the Fates permit," "Golden Bough."

5. Transformation, change, alteration, mutation.

_____ Questions for Review _____

1. No.

2. They altered, reworked, amplified, moralized, systematized, and recorded them.

3. By direct or indirect inspiration of Apollo or the Muses.

4. Homer, the *Iliad* and the *Odyssey*; Hesiod, *Works and Days* and *Origin of the Gods* (*Theogony*).

5. His versions of many of the myths became the "received" versions.

6. In whatever way their inspiration led them; with great freedom.

7. They systematized, reinterpreted, and transmitted them; a few they invented.

8. Virgil, *Aeneid*; Ovid, *Metamorphoses, Fasti, Epistolae Heroidum*.

9. In his patriotism, his respect for the old ways, and his introduction of Roman gods and their stories into his epic.

10. He made them into a prologue to the greatness of Rome.

11. Most of the Greek gods (often with their Roman names) and a number of Roman ones.

12. "*Timeo Danaos et dona ferentes,*" "*facilis descensus Averno,*" etc.

13. They appear directly in their own forms or in disguise; they speak through signs, oracles, and dreams.

14. A special bough which Aeneas had to find as a gift for Proserpina before he could enter the Lower World.

15. It purports to deal with all the stories of transformations, which include nearly all the myths known to us.

16. More than two hundred.

17. He has recorded for us more myths than any other writer of antiquity.

PART TWO:
OTHER MYTHS OF THE
OLD WORLD

18   Gods of the Northland

Creation of the World

The complex and grotesque cosmogony of the North is much more typical of the mythological cosmogonies of most cultures than is the more philosophical, somewhat allegorized Greek version. It is unusual, however, in its picture of a developing multiple universe consisting eventually of nine separate universes or worlds, all but two of which are destroyed in the end.

    Two of these, Gimle and Vanaheim, do not appear in the cosmogony: their origins are not given; they are simply there. *Vanaheim* ("Home of the Vanir") was the original dwelling-place of Frey and Freya, who belonged to the *Vanir*, a race of gods not related to the *Aesir*, the descendants of Buri. Modern scholars believe that the Vanir, who were all fertility gods, belonged to a bronze-age culture which had migrated north from a warmer climate, bringing its gods along. Later the nomadic iron-age warrior-culture of the Norsemen invaded these lands, bringing the Aesir, their gods of storm and battle. The story that some of the Vanir joined the Aesir in Asgard suggests that there was a combining of the cults, just as in Greece at an earlier period the Earth-Mother had been admitted into the cult of the Sky-Father. The Vanir were the gods of rain and soft winds, not of gales and storms.

    Gimle ("Jeweled Roof") was the highest heaven, the home of Alfadur ("Father of All"), who came after Ragnarok ("Destiny of the Gods") to found a new Midgard, peopling it from the offspring of the only two human survivors. Gimle and Alfadur may have come into the cosmology of the Norse along with Christianity, as an attempt to fit the new God into the existing framework.

At the beginning of time two of the worlds were already in existence: Niflheim ("Home of Fog"), filled with ice from the freezing of its ten rivers, and Muspellsheim ("Home of Destruction"), filled with fire. Niflheim was later to become the dwelling-place of Nidhogg ("Hateful"), the dragon who gnawed at the root of Yggdrasil, and of Hel and her followers, as well as of all the dead who had died of disease or old age. Muspellsheim was to be the home of the fire-demons and Surt ("Black"), their lord.

Betwen Niflheim and Muspellsheim lay the Norse version of Chaos, Ginungagap ("Gaping Confusion"), not another world but a pit into which crept the fire and ice of the adjacent worlds. The people of the cold north thought of life as created by warmth (not by breath, like the Hebrews, Greeks, and Romans). The steam caused by the meeting of the fire and ice created Ymir and Aduhumla. The first pair of Giants were born from the warm armpit of the sleeping Ymir, and the first Troll from his feet. Similarly, it was the warmth of Audhumla's tongue which brought Buri into being as she licked the ice. The rim of Ginungagap was soon populated with many Jotunns ("Devourers"), most of whom were Giants or Trolls, but some of whose females were of ordinary size and great beauty: the wives of both Buri and Bor were Jotunn maidens.

When they first slew Ymir, the three Aesir pushed his body from the rim into Ginungagap. The brine which flowed from his wounds filled the pit and overflowed its rim, drowning Audhumla and all the Jotunns but two, a male and female who got onto an ice floe and drifted to the shore of this new sea, a region of mountains and glaciers which became Jotunnheim ("Home of the Devourers"). They populated Jotunnheim with their descendants, the Frost-Giants and Trolls. The Giants had heads of stone and feet of ice, but were otherwise like men except for their gigantic size. Some of them could change themselves into wolves or eagles. The Trolls were not only gigantic but ugly and monstrous, often having more than one head (the wife of the Giant Hymir had nine hundred). Hence the Jotunns of the Norsemen bear a really startling resemblance to the Giants of the Greeks.

The next world to be created was Midgard ("Middle Enclosure"), made by the Aesir from Ymir's body after they had hauled it from the sea. To keep Midgard from being frozen they thrust Niflheim deep into the earth; to prevent it from burning they set the sky, Ymir's skull, between Midgard and Muspellsheim. Some of Muspellsheim's fire they set in the sky but, since the sun and the moon did not move, there was no day and night until the three Aesir made them wagons drawn by pairs of horses. The sun's horses had bellows attached to their flanks to cool them and keep them from being burnt. Two Jotunns, in the form of wolves, pursued these wagons across the sky hoping to swallow the sun and moon, since Jotunns hated the light.

The three Aesir next created the Light Elves. These were beautiful winged creatures, kindly and good. The magic belts which they wore inspired love in any who saw them; they also had cloaks of invisibility. For them the Aesir created the seventh world, Alfheim ("Home of the Elves") high above Midgard.

For the dwarves, whom they had made to mine gold, silver, and iron for them, they created the underground world of Darkalfheim ("Home of the Dark Elves"). Like the Greek Hephaestus, these Dark Elves were able to make wonderful things of metal. They made Frya's light-producing necklace, the solid gold hair of Thor's wife Sif, Odin's spear Gungnir ("Sounding") which never missed, the flying ship Skidbladner ("Made of Wooden Slats") which could carry all the gods but could also be folded up small enough to put into a pouch, the golden boar on which Frey rode through the sky, Thor's hammer Mjolnir ("Flashing Crusher") which flew back to his hand when he had thrown it, and Odin's bracelet Draupnir ("Dripping") which produced eight more bracelets like itself every ninth night.

The ninth and last world to be created was Asgard ("Enclosure of the Aesir"). Its center was the open field of Ida ("Place of Activity") where the gods amused themselves playing chess on golden boards. Here also the dead heroes of Valhalla practised warfare in preparation for Ragnarok, cutting each other in pieces and then being reassembled in time for the next meal. Ida was the only area not destroyed in the final battle. Around Ida stood the thirteen halls of the gods: Valhalla, the hall of the heroes; Gladsheim, which held the thrones of Odin and the twelve principal gods; Vingolf, with the thrones of Frigg and the Asynjer (female Aesir); Bilskirnir, Thor's hall, in his district of Thruthvang; Ydalir, the hall of Ull; Soekkva-bekk, Saga's hall; Breithablik, Balder's hall; Sessrymnir, the hall of Freya in her district of Folkvang where she entertained half the heroes; Noatun, the hall of Njord; Thrymheim, Skade's hall; Glitnir, the justice-hall of Forseti; Himinbjorg, Heimdall's hall; and Vithi, the hall of Vidar. Above these towered Odin's silver tower, Valaskjalf. Sitting on his throne Lidskjalf ("Gate Tower") on the top of this tower, he could see the whole world and all that happened in it. Around the outside of Asgard was a fence with posts of gold and silver rails.

Each of the roots of Yggdrasil was watered by a different spring. The one in Asgard was tended by the Norns, who used its water to water the tree, a task they carried out with great care. The water of the one in Niflheim, however, was drunk by the dragon Nidhogg which constantly gnawed at the root and eventually, on the day of Ragnarok, killed the tree. The spring in Jotunnheim was called Mimir's Well; it contained all the wisdom of the Jotunns. It was tended by a Jotunn named Mimir ("Pondering") who drank from it every morning and so was very wise. Wanting to share this wisdom, Odin asked Mimir for a drink from the well. Mimir agreed only on condition that Odin would share with him his ability to see all things. So Odin had to give Mimir one of his eyes, which Mimir hid in the well. Looking down into the eye, he could see the whole world and all that took place in it. Mimir became Odin's trusted advisor.

The gifts which the three gods gave to Ask and Embla were appropriate to their natures: Odin means "Spirit," Lodur (Ve's name in the prose Edda) "Flame," and Vili "Will." The Norse, unlike most peoples, did not picture the first state of mankind as a kind of Golden Age from which man had degenerated. In Norse mythology the first men were clumsy uncouth savages living in hovels and wearing the skins of animals, very much like our picture of cavemen. Only as generations passed did man, taught by Odin who often visited Midgard in disguise, learn the refinements of civilization. Later, as wars increased, mankind began to go downhill again but its decadence was interrupted by Ragnarok.

Gods of the North

Most of the male Aesir were sons or grandsons of Odin; the only important exceptions were Njord, Frey, and Loki. Balder ("Lord") was his son by his favorite wife, Frigg ("Lady"); Balder's wife Nanna ("Mother") was famous for her constancy, voluntarily accompanying her husband to the realm of Hel. Their son Forseti ("Presider") was the chief judge of the Aesir.

Thor ("Thunder") was Odin's son by the Jotunn Erda ("Earth"); Thor's wife Sif ("Kinship"), the goddess of the household and family ties, was the mother of Ull ("Shaggy"), the god of skiing. Thor and Sif also had two sons Modi ("Courageous") and Magni ("Strength"). Like Hercules, Magni was, even in infancy, stronger than any god except his father. He and his brother Modi were two of the seven Aesir who survived Ragnarok.

Tyr ("Shining") was borne to Odin by a daughter of the Jotunn Hymir.

Odin's son Heimdall ("Rainbow"), the guardian of the bridge Bifrost, was unique among gods and men in having solid gold teeth and nine mothers. These were the beautiful daughters of the Jotunn Aegir ("Sea") and his wife Ran ("Plunder"). Aegir, who was the god of stormy seas, would sink ships with the help of his daughters, who were the waves; then Ran would ransack the wrecks for gold.

By the Jotunn woman Grid ("Peace"), Ovid became the father of the war-gods Vidar ("Wide-Ruling") and Vali ("Terrible"). Vali was the youngest of the Aesir. His brother Vidar had as his battle-weapon an enormous boot made from scraps of leather which were left over when good men in Midgard made their own booths. Vali and Vidar both survived Ragnarok.

Two other war-gods, Hoethr ("War") and Hermod ("Courage in Battle"), were Odin's sons by other Jotunn women. Hoethr, who was blind, was the god of brute force unguided by reason.

Adventures of the Gods

The stories of Njord, Frey, Freya, and Bragi are connected with the Vanir. One of the Vanir, Gullveig ("Power of Gold"), a very beautiful goddess, had come to Asgard in search of gold. When the Aesir began to quarrel among themselves and to vie with each other in making gifts of gold to her, Odin saw that she was evil and attempted to burn her at the stake. Each time she was burned she rose from the flames in a different shape; so after three attempts Odin let her go. She complained to the Vanir that she had been mistreated. In their anger they broke into Asgard and fought the Aesir on the plain of Ida. The battle was a draw, so peace was made and hostages were exchanged. The Vanir Njord and his two children, Frey and Freya, came as hostages to the Aesir. Odin gave to the Vanir his own brother Vili and his adviser Mimir. Njord was the god who gave fair winds and put out destructive fires; he later married the Jotunn Skade, the goddess of skiing.

Because he was Odin's brother Vili became the ruler of the Vanir, who were delighted with his wise judgements; but when they realized that he always consulted the wise Mimir they became angry, assuming that he was stupid and that Odin had cheated them by sending a hostage of no value. In their anger they beheaded Mimir and sent his head to Odin, who kept it in his hall and consulted it in times of trouble.

When the Aesir and Vanir had exchanged their hostages they sealed the peace treaty by ritually chewing berries and spitting the juice into the same large tub. From the juices was born Kvasir ("Saliva"), the god of knowledge and of drunkenness. Since he knew everything and was able to answer any question he became a kind of oracle for the Aesir; but two of the Dark Elves, wanting this knowledge for themselves, crept into Asgard, drowned Kvasir in the tub, then carried it off to Darkalfheim. They set up three kettles, added honey, and made mead with the juice. Anyone who drank this mead would be inspired and speak in poetry. The kettles were taken from the dwarves by a Jotunn named Suttung who hid them in a cave and entrusted them to the care of his beautiful daughter Gunnlod. All-seeing Odin knew where the mead was hidden; so, disguising himself as a handsome young man, he came to Gunnlod and so won her heart that after three days she agreed to let him take one drink from each kettle. With each drink he emptied a kettle, then turned himself into an eagle to fly back to Asgard, with Suttung, also in the form of an eagle, in hot pursuit.

Heimdall, seeing the birds approaching, had the Aesir bring out all the vessels they had. They did this just in time for Odin to spit the mead out into them. This was the mead which from then on was Odin's only nourishment. He let the other gods each have a little and he gave some occasionally to men of Midgard, who thus became great poets.

Odin regretted the deception he had practised on Gunnlod and, when he saw that she had had a son by him, he brought the boy, Bragi ("Song"), to Asgard and made him one of the gods. Like the Greek Hercules, Bragi was married to the goddess of youth, Ithunn ("Rejuvenation"), the keeper of the Apples of Youth.

Several of the Jotunns were, like Aegir, on good terms with the Aesir, and many Jotunn women were inhabitants of Asgard. Loki ("Fire"), however, was the only male Jotunn who dwelt in Asgard on equal terms with the Aesir. This was because he was Odin's blood-brother. In his youth, Odin had been struck by the cleverness of the handsome young Jotunn. Mingling their blood they had sworn always to come to each other's defense, and that neither would ever accept any boon which was not offered to the other. Loki's wife in Asgard was Sigunn ("Giver of Victory"), who was faithful to her untrustworthy husband to the end. When Loki was punished for the death of Balder, Sigunn sat by him catching in a cup the serpent's venom which would have dripped onto his face. It was only when she had to empty the cup that a drop would fall on him and he would writhe in agony; this was the cause of earthquakes.

In Jotunnheim Loki had another wife, Angerboda ("Anguish-Bringer"). By her he became the father of Fenrir, Hel, and the Midgard Serpent.

Besides Nanna, Ithun, Sif, Skade, and Sigunn, there were other goddesses who gathered around Frigg in Vingolf. There were her three attendants, Fulla ("Cup-Bearer"), Gna ("Bounteous"), and Lin ("Head-Dress"). Gna had a marvelous horse which ran so fast that it could cross over the sea without wetting its feet. She was Frigg's messenger, as Iris was Juno's. Lin watched over Frigg's favorites in Midgard and Fulla shared her secrets. Eir ("Mercy") was the goddess of health, Var ("Truth") was the goddess of oaths between men and women, and punished oath-breakers, Saga ("Story") inspired seeresses in Midgard, and Gefjon ("Giving") carried Frigg's gifts to women. A hank of yarn from Frigg, for example, would never run out in the weaving.

Frey's wife Gerd ("Enclosure") was sometimes found in the group of goddesses who surrounded Frigg though her home was with her husband in Alfheim. Gerd, the daughter of a frost giant, was the most beautiful of all women but it had been thought that she would never marry since her heart was frozen and she could not love. Although Odin allowed no one but Frigg to sit on Lidskjalf, Frey had once tried it briefly, had seen Gerd in her father's hall and had fallen in love. Frey's unrequited love for Gerd, like Ceres' grief for Proserpina, caused the earth to become barren. She finally agreed to marry him and when they met her heart melted, as the ice of winter gives way to the warmth of spring.

Frey's sister Freya was not often found with the other goddesses. She remains a rather mysterious figure in some ways. Her name, a variant of Frigg's (they both mean "Lady,"—really a title of respect rather than a name), suggests that she was the chief goddess of the Vanir. Her husband's name was Od, a variant of Odin's name. Perhaps this pair had been the Jupiter and Juno of the Vanir pantheon, displaced by Odin and Frigg. Od was thought of as having disappeared before Freya came to Asgard; remembering him Freya would sometimes weep golden tears. Freya helped Odin entertain the fighting men whom he was gathering about him in preparation for Ragnarok.

These heroes were the ones who had been brought to Asgard by the Valkyries ("Choosers of Fallen Warriors"), whose function was to watch battles, select the bravest heroes, and bring them away when they were killed, to swell the host which Odin was building up for the final battle. A warrior who felt that he had been chosen by a Valkyrie would of course kill as many of the enemy as he could before he died, knowing that he was headed for Valhalla ("Hall of Fallen Warriors"), where the time was spent joyously feasting, sleeping, and fighting. Valhalla was very large: it had five hundred and forty doors, each wide enough to admit a thousand men abreast. Its walls were of spears and its roof of shields; on the roof were a golden cock which crowed every morning and a magical goat whose udder flowed with mead. This mead streamed down through the roof and into kettles, and was so plentiful that there was always enough for all the heroes. The feasting in Valhalla was presided over by Odin and the four wargods, his sons Tyr, Hothr, Vidar, and Vali.

Death of Balder

After the death of Balder and the imprisonment of Loki the hostile Jotunns grew bolder; the earth grew colder until finally there was only winter. After three years of this, during which Nighogg completed the destruction of one of Yggdrasil's roots, the day of Ragnarok was signaled by the crowing of the golden cock of Valhalla and the black cock of Hel. At the death of the great ash tree the Norns, who watered its Midgard root, stopped spinning the thread of life. At the same time all the evils which the Aesir had imprisoned broke free. The three children of Loki—Hel, Fenrir, and the Midgard Serpent—and Loki himself were all freed. Loki came riding in a magical ship full of evil ghosts. This ship Nagelfar ("Nail-Traveler"), was made of the fingernails of the dead. To delay its building and the day of Ragnarok, the nails of the dead were always trimmed before their funerals. The din of the fighting split the sky and Surt and his Fire-Demons streamed out of Muspellsheim through the cracks.

Fire-demons, evil ghosts, Jotunns, and monsters clashed with the Aesir on the field of Vigrid, a hundred miles in each dimension. Thor fought and killed the Midgard Serpent, but died himself from the venom which the serpent vomited onto him as it died. Tyr killed Hel's watchdog Garm (the Norse Cerberus) but died from the wounds he had received. Surt killed Frey with his flaming sword. Loki and Heimdall killed each other. Odin attacked Fenrir but was swallowed by him; Vidar then killed Fenrir by thrusting his immense boot into the wolf's jaws. When all of Odin's warriors and all but seven of the Aesir had been killed, the Jotunn wolves swallowed the sun and the moon, the stars fell from the sky, Midgard and Asgard were devastated by fire and earthquakes, and Midgard then sank beneath the sea. In the end there was only the field of Ida and a few survivors: Balder and Hothr (who had escaped from Hel when all the bonds had been loosed), Thor's sons Magni and Modi, Odin's sons Vidar and Vali, Vili (who came back from Vanaheim to join them), and the goddesses.

There were also two human survivors, Lif and Lifthrasir, who under the new rays of the old sun's daughter, began a new world under the care of Alfadur of Gimle.

PRACTICAL APPLICATIONS

_____ References to Mythology in Literature _____

1. The world of the Aesir.

2. Wife of Odin and queen of the gods.

3. The mistletoe was the only thing in the world which had not sworn not to harm Balder; it was the mistletoe that killed him.

4. God of thunder, whose weapon was the hammer.

5. The Norns, the Norse Fates.

6. Balder was the best and most beautiful of the gods, a son of Odin and Frigg.

7. King and father of the Aesir.

8. *Weird Sisters* is a title given also to the Norns.

9. Odin's hall where he feasted his fallen warriors.

11. The goddess of love.

12. Odin was the king of the Aesir.

13. The maidens who went out to choose the bravest men of Midgard for Odin's army.

14. Thor was the god of thunder.

15. Hoder (Hothr, Hod) was the blind god of war.

16. The Norns, who knew the future and spun the threads of life, were the Norse Fates.

_____ Word Study _____

1. Tiu's (Tyr's) day; Woden's (Odin's) day; Thor's day; Freya's day. By comparison with the Romance names for the days we can see that Tyr was equated with Mars, Odin with Mercury, Thor with Jupiter, and Freya with Venus. You might ask your class why these particular identifications were made. Thor, rather than Odin, took Jupiter's day because they are both gods of thunder; Odin was like Mercury in his quick wit.

3. In Scotland _weird_ still mean "fate;" the English meaning comes from such usages as Shakespeare's "weird sisters:" because witches were seeresses, "weird" came to mean "witchlike."

4. Skuld, whose name means either "future" or "duty;" the toast may mean either "your future" or "my duty (to you)." (Some scholars believe, however, that it comes from _skaal_, "drinking-bowl.") _Valhalla_ means "Hall of Heroes." Letters used by the Norse for writing their language. Minstrel, bard, poet, gleeman, mastersinger.

_____ Questions for Review _____

1. The northern gods include more, and more important gods of war, wintry cold, and storms, and fewer and less important gods of agriculture. The northern gods are more serious and dutiful. Also, they are mortal.

2. It was created by the three gods Odin, Vili, and Ve from the body of the giant Ymir.

3. The stars were sparks from Muspellsheim, set in the sky by the three gods; they also created the sun and the moon.

4. At the foot of the great ash-tree Yggdrasill.

5. Three sisters, the Norse version of the Greek Fates, who watered a root of Yggdrasill and spun the threads of life.

6. Odin.

7. Asgard.

8. Frigg.

9. The mead of knowledge.

10. The Choosers of the Slain, warrior maidens who brought the bravest of the dead heroes to Asgard.

11. Thor.

12. A hammer which would return to his hand when thrown, iron mittens to catch it with, and the Girdle of Strength.

13. God of sunlight, spring, and gladness; god of fertility, sunshine, soft rain, and harvests; goddess of love, music, and flowers, one of the war-gods; god of poetry; goddess of youth and early spring; the blind god of war and winter; god of skiing, ice-skating, and archery; god of justice.

14. Loki; Hel

15. With a magical chain made by the Dark Elves. Tyr had to place his hand in Fenrir's mouth as a pledge, so that he would allow himself to be bound.

16. His marvelous horse was lured into the forest [by Loki, in the shape of a mare, which later gave birth to Odin's eight-legged horse Sleipnir.]

17. He fought with them with his hammer. In the hall of Utgard-Loki he contended in drinking and wrestling.

18. Hoethr, at the prompting of Loki, shot him with a mistletoe arrow.

19. Most of them would die.

21. The Judgement (or Destiny) of the Gods.

19   Heroes of the North

Siegfried

There are a number of differing accounts of this hero, both among the Germans, who call him Siegfried, and among the Norse, who call him Sigurd. The two chief stories are the Norse *Saga of the Volsungs* and the German *Song of the Nibelungs*, but he also appears in several poems of the Elder Edda. The story given in the text is essentially that of the *Nibelungenlied.*

In the Norse story Sigurd's ancestry, like that of the Greek heroes, was divine. He was the son of Sigmund the son of Volsung, whose father, Rerir, was the son of Odin's son Sigi. Rerir's wife was barren and conceived Volsung only after eating an apple which Odin had given her.

On one of his visits to Midgard, Odin had come in disguise to the Hall of Volsung and had plunged a great sword into the living ash tree which supported the Hall as Yggdrasil supported the universe. This was a test of readiness, like Theseus' sword under the stone or Arthur's sword in the stone. As each of the sons of Volsung grew up he attempted to remove the sword, but only the last, Sigmund, was able to do so.

While Sigmund was still a boy, the husband of his elder sister Signy treacherously killed Volsung and took his sons captive. Since they were his brothers by marriage he could not kill them himself; but he took them one at a time to the forest, tied them up, and left them, and they were eaten by wolves. Signy managed to save Sigmund, who was the last, and made him swear to avenge their father and brothers. Signy knew that he could not do this alone but, since they were the only surviving Volsungs, there was no one to help him. So when Sigmund had grown and acquired his sword she visited him in disguise and by him became the mother of Sinfiotli, whom she sent to live with his father until he should be grown. In the meantime she gave her husband no hint of her desire for vengeance, so when Sinfiotli grew up, he and Sigmund were able to take him by surprise. They killed his and Signy's children while she looked on, then shut her husband in his hall and set fire to it. After telling Sigmund that vengeance was now satisfied, she went into the hall and died with her husband.

With his divine unbreakable sword Sigmund fought bravely for many years, until it was time for him to join the heroes in Valhalla. Then Odin himself met him in battle and shattered his sword with his magical spear. He was wounded but, when his wife Hijoerdis came to bind up his wounds, he refused treatment, knowing that he had been called by Odin.

He merely asked his wife to give the fragments of his sword to their son Sigurd.

Once when Odin was traveling through Midgard accompanied, as he often was, by Vili and Loki, they came upon an otter who had just caught a salmon. Loki threw a stone and killed the otter, boasting that with one stone he had acquired both an otter and a salmon. Loki and Vili ate both and took the skin of the otter with them when they moved on. They lodged at night with Hreidmar, who realized that the skin belonged to his son, who had transformed himself into an otter. Hreidmar and his other two sons, Fafnir and Regin, bound the three gods as they slept. They would not release them until they had promised to pay the death price for the dead man by covering the otter-skin with so much gold that none of it could be seen. Loki was released to go in search of the gold.

The Dark Elf Andvari, a cunning miner and smith, had a great treasure, but he was hard to catch because he was able to shift his shape. Loki finally managed to discover him swimming in a river in the form of a fish (the same device Loki himself was later to use when the Aesir were hunting him for his part in the death of Balder). He caught the fish, and Andvari was forced (like the Roman Incubo or a leprechaun) to disclose the location of the gold. He tried to keep back one gold ring, a magical talisman which brought great wealth to its owner, but Loki took that as well, even though Andvari put a curse on it and warned him that it would eventually destroy its possessor.

When Loki returned Odin wanted to keep the ring; but it was needed to cover the last whisker of the otter-skin, and he was forced to leave it with the rest of the gold. The curse of the ring began to work when Fafnir and Regin killed their father for the treasure. Fafnir then stole Regin's share from him and, when Regin came to retrieve it, turned himself into a dragon.

Unable to kill Fafnir, Regin, who was a skilled smith, came to Sigurd and offered to reforge Sigmund's sword if Sigurd would promise to do a favor for him afterward. Sigurd agreed and accompanied Regin to his forge where he stayed until the sword was mended. Then Regin sent him to kill Fafnir, warning him that the dragon was invulnerable except in the belly and instructing him to hide in a pit and thrust upward when Fafnir crawled over it. When he had killed the dragon he was to cut out its heart and roast it for Regin to eat.

While roasting the heart Sigurd touched it and burnt his thumb, which he automatically put into his mouth. As soon as the juices of the heart touched his tongue he found that he could understand the speech of birds. From the conversation of two nuthatches in a nearby tree he learned that Regin intended to kill him on his return with the treasure; so he cut off the smith's head and kept the gold, including the fatal ring, for himself.

The Valkyrie Brynhild had disobeyed Odin by giving victory in battle to a king whom he had wanted to die. Odin told her that in punishment he would put her into a magical sleep, to be taken by the first man who came to wake her. She begged him at least to ensure that the man would be a brave one; so he surrounded her sleeping-place with a ring of fire. Though he didn't tell her, he went further than this: he gave to Sigurd the horse Grani, sired by his own marvelous horse, the eight-legged Sleipnir, foal of Svadilfari and Loki in the guise of a mare.

Mounted on Grani, Sigurd leapt the wall of fire and woke Brynhild; they fell in love and she became his bride. When after three days he went adventuring, he gave her the fatal ring and left her still protected by the fire. Coming to the country of the Giukungs, Sigurd swore blood-brotherhood with their king Gunnar. Seeing the hero's prowess, Gunnar's mother Griemhild, who was something of a witch, decided that she wanted him to marry her daughter Gudrun. So she gave him a magic potion which caused him to forget Brynhild's very existence, and he asked Gunnar for Gudrun's hand. Ironically, Gunnar promised him his sister only on the condition that he would win for him the hand of a beautiful Valkyrie who was sleeping within a wall of fire — Brynhild herself. Gunnar was not brave enough to accomplish this quest himself. By her magic powers Griemhild gave Sigurd the appearance of Gunnar and, disguised in this way, he rode once again through the ring of fire and awoke Brynhild. She did not love this apparent stranger but was forced by the conditions of her punishment to accept him as her husband.

Again Sigurd remained three nights with her but this time he placed his sword between them in the bed. When he came back with her to the Giukungs the reaL Gunnar took his place, and Sigurd, restored to his own form by Griemhild, returned to Gudrun. Seeing that Sigurd had forgotten her and had married another, Brynhild assumed that he was unfaithful to her and settled down with Gunnar, who was at least (she thought) a brave enough man to have ridden through the flames for her.

But Gudrun knew the truth about Gunnar's wooing and revealed it to Brynhild in the course of a quarrel. To get her revenge on Sigurd for this double insult (for Gudrun had not revealed that it was by magic that Sigurd had been made to forget her), Brynhild lied to Gunnar, telling him that Sigurd had broken his oath and had not placed his sword between them during the three nights which they had spent together. She swore that she would leave him if he did not kill Sigurd.

Gunnar could not kill a blood-brother, but he persuaded his younger brother to kill Sigurd while he was sleeping. Having thus accomplished her revenge, Brynhild killed herself, but before she died she begged that she be placed on the funeral pyre with Sigurd. And so she followed him to Hel.

Odin retrieved the ring from the pyre but its baleful influence continued. Gunnar gave Gudrun in marriage to Atli, a neighboring king, who invited her brothers to visit his hall and then killed them, as Signy's husband had killed her brothers. Gudrun avenged their deaths by killing Atli's children by her and then Atli himself.

Students who are familiar with Wagner's *Ring* cycle will see that he has combined the Norse and German stories for his plot. A comparison of Wagner's version with either story, or of the two stories with each other, could make an interesting report.

Beowulf

Just as the *Nibelungenlied* is a German reworking of Norse mythology, so Beowulf is an English version of a Norse story, one of the best pieces of Anglo-Saxon literature. It dates from the xith Century.

Even before he went to Denmark to help Hrothgar, Beowulf had performed feats rivaling those of the Greek Hercules. As a boy he swam from his native land of Sweden to Finland, taking seven days and seven nights and killing many sea-monsters on his way. Once after a battle he swam to his ship carrying the armor of thirty men whom he had killed.

When he came of age he was offered the throne of his native land but refused it, becoming the advisor and protector of the young king Heardred. He accepted the throne only after his return from Denmark, when Heardred had died.

Beowulf's name, "Bee-Wolf," means "Bear." The men of the north thought the bear the bravest of animals; they would sometimes try to acquire the bear's courage by wearing robes of bearskin. Such a robe was called a *berserk* ("bear-sark"; the word *sark*, meaning "shirt," is still current in Scotland). Their frenzied courage gave the word the meaning it has today.

PRACTICAL APPLICATIONS

_____ Specific Literary References _____

1. The Norse hero of an Anglo-Saxon poem, the slayer of Grendel and his dam and of a fire-breathing dragon.

2. The reference is to Beowulf's killing of the dragon which was devastating his land in revenge for the theft of part of its treasure.

3. The monstrous mother of the monstrous Grendel, whose arm Beowulf had torn off, so that he died.

4. Wiglaf reproaches his companions for refusing to follow King Beowulf in pursuit of the dragon.

5. Dwarves who were skilled smiths.

6. Brunhild was the queen of Iceland who came to Burgundy to marry King Gunther.

7. The reference is to the bear which Siegfried captured for a prank to frighten Mimer.

_____ Questions for Review _____

1. The Netherlands.

2. Mimer's.

3. Dwarves who were skillful smiths.

4. Strength, courage, a rather Germanic sense of humor.

5. Having aroused it with a blast on his horn, he muzzled it with his belt and used it to frighten Mimer.

6. By constantly shattering his anvil and by playing tricks on him.

7. By sending him where he would meet the dragon Fafnir.

8. The dragon Fafnir.

9. By bathing in the dragon's blood.

10. He killed him.

11. The Queen of Iceland.

12. Indifference.

13. By agreeing to arbitrate a dispute over it among the Nibelungs, then losing his temper and killing them all.

14. He must help her brother Gunther to win Brunhild.

15. By donning his cloak of invisibility and helping Gunther to pass Brunhild's tests.

16. Brunhild had learned of his vulnerable spot from his wife Kriemhild. She told his secret enemy Hagen, who persuaded Kriemhild to embroider on his garment a cross marking the spot, so that Hagen would be better able to protect him in battle. Then he killed him.

17. She killed Hagen.

18. Those of Hrothgar, King of the Danes.

19. The land of the Goths (Geats), in what is now southern Sweden.
20. He tore off Grendel's arm.
21. By following her to her underwater den and killing her there.
22. With many rich gifts.
23. A fire-breathing dragon.
24. He killed the dragon but died himself from the flames.

20   Celtic Fairyland

The Ancient Celts

The Celts were called "Gauls" (*Galli*) by the Romans and "Galatians" (*Galatoi*) by the Greeks; the Galatians to whom St. Paul wrote his epistle were a small group left behind in Asia Minor during the great westward migration. The Romans found the Gauls, unlike the Germans, very amenable to Roman civilization; the Gauls admired Roman ways so much that in many parts of their territory they abandoned their own language and spoke Latin instead. Their language survives today as Cymric in Wales where it is widely spoken, Gaelic in Scotland where it is a living language in the more remote districts, and Erse in Ireland where it is the official language of the republic, taught in the schools but not really in everyday use.

Celtic Gods

Our information about the Celtic gods is scanty because the Celts did not believe in committing sacred matters to writing; instead, they were memorized and passed down through generations by word of mouth. We must turn to comments of outside observers and to inscriptions on statues and other dedications for our information.

As we have seen, the Romans, thinking their own gods universal, readily identified the gods of other cultures with their own. The Greek gods are the prime objects of this tendency, but it was applied also to the gods of the near east and of the north. Among the Gauls this identification, like everything that was Roman, met with a ready acceptance and the Gauls began depicting their own gods with Roman attributes and Roman gods with the attributes of Celtic gods. Hence we find a figure clad in a lion's skin and carrying a club, clearly Hercules, inscribed with the name *Ogmios*, which belongs to a Celtic god. Similarly, there are statuettes of Jupiter carrying the usual Roman version of a thunderbolt (a bundle of flames and arrows tied together in the middle) but also carrying the Celtic version of a thunderbolt, an S-shaped double spiral, as well as the wheel which is the attribute of the Celtic thunder-god Taranis. As further evidence of this strange sycretism there are depictions which show Roman gods and Celtic gods together: in one relief of Lugh and his mother (?)

Rosmerta, Rosmerta holds her Celtic attributes of cornucopia and winnowing-fan, but Lugh holds the caduceus and purse, and wears the winged sandals and cap of Mercury.

This identification with Roman gods ought to make it easy to learn the functions and relationships of the Celtic gods, but an unknown factor is the degree of understanding which the Romans and the Gauls may have had of each other's divinities. We have seen that Roman syncretisms were often superficial, relying on only a few details of the god's functions and/or appearance. For example, Astarte was worshipped by the Romans as Juno, Diana, and Venus in different places. Another complication lies in the fact that the Celts appear not to have had universal gods, so that the same functions may be exercised by different gods in different tribes. It also sometimes happens that a god of the same name will be assigned different functions by different tribes.

The earliest historical information we have about the Gallic gods comes from Julius Caesar, who says in his commentaries:

Their principal god is Mercury, of whom there are numerous images up and down Gaul: he is regarded as inventor of all the arts; the god who points the road and guides the traveler's footsteps; the great patron of trade and riches. After Mercury come Apollo, Mars, Jupiter, and Minerva, about all of whom they have much the same ideas as other nations: Apollo averts disease, Minerva teaches the elements of industry and handicrafts, Jupiter rules the sky, Mars presides over war . . . The Gauls claim . . . that their whole race is descended from Dis, lord of the underworld.

That Caesar's identifications are not superficial is proven by the fact that he does not make the easy syncretism of the "principal god" with Jupiter, but has looked more closely at the actual functions of the gods. Celtic names for these gods in the order in which he lists them are Lugh, Grannus, Teutates, Taranis, and Brigit. Dis (Pluto) is Donn, a male counterpart of Dana. Inscriptions on statues and reliefs offer some variants: Minerva is sometimes Sulis, a goddess of thermal springs, and hence of healing; Apollo is sometimes Belenus or Borvo, gods of thermal springs, or Maponus, the harper god; Dis is sometimes Cernunnos, the horned master of wild animals. Inscriptions also provide other identifications: Vulcan with Gofannon (Gobban), the smith god, Maia with Rosemerta, a goddess of abundance, Silvanus with Sucellus, the hammer god, and Hercules with Ogmios, the strong champion of the gods. There are a number of other gods whose names we know and whose functions we can deduce but no others have yet been found to have been syncretized with Greco-Roman gods.

Lucan calls Teutates, Esus, and Taranis cruel because they all received human sacrifices: those to Teutates were drowned by being plunged head first into a vat; those to Esus were hung on a tree and wounded so that they bled to death; those to Taranis were enclosed in large wicker-work images and burnt alive.

Celtic Cycles of Legends

The Celts had no scruples about committing to writing their "history"; hence we have many legends of heroes, but no myths of gods.

The *Book of Invasions* (*Leabhar Gabhala*) compiled in the xiith Century provides legendary descriptions of seven invasions of Ireland, the first dating from before the Flood and led by a granddaughter of Noah.

The Ultonian (from *Ulaidh*, "Ulstermen") or Conorian (from *Conor*, a modern spelling and pronunciation of *Conchobhar mac Nessa*, the name of its hero) Cycle dates from the viith Century but describes events purporting to have taken place at about the beginning of our era. This was the Heroic Age of Celtic legend and the stories of this cycle were popular among the lords of the land.

The third of the Cycles was much more popular with the lower classes. Dating from the xiiith Century, it gradually replaced the Ultonian Cycle in popularity, and some of its stories are still current in Irish story-telling today. It is called "Ossianic" and "Fenian" from its heroes, Fen (*Fionn*) and his son Ossian (*Oisin*).

All of these works come from Ireland, along with a few isolated tales and a fourth work, the xiith-Century "History of Places" (*Dinnshenchas*), which provides some details of myth and legend in its aetiological explanations of Irish place-names.

The Welsh *Mabinogion* ("Instructions to the Young," i.e. material to be learned by the bards' apprentices) consist of eleven separate works. The first four of these are called "the Four Branches;" these date from the xith Century. They are: First Branch, *Pwyll and Pryderi*; Second Branch, *Branwen Daughter of Llyr*; Third Branch, *Manawyddan*; and Fourth Branch, *Math Son of Mathonwy*.

These are the Mabinogion proper; the other seven works, which were added to it in the xivth Century, all have to do with King Arthur, some of whose exploits had been told in the xth-Century Welsh poem *The Spoils of Annwn* and in the xith-Century Welsh tale *Culhwch and Olwen*. Neither of these was included in the Mabinogion.

Cycle of the Invasions

The First Invasion was led by a woman, Cesair, daughter of Noah's son Bith. This invasion was interrupted by the Flood. The only survivor was one Fintan, who lived through the other six invasions and was supposed to be the source of information about them.

In the Second Invasion Partholan and his followers fought the demons known as the Fomhoire or Fomorians, some of whom had only one foot and one eye each. Partholan created four plains and seven lakes in Ireland, established many of the legal and religious customs of the land, and introduced the brewing of beer and ale. He and his followers were killed by a plague.

Nemed, the invader of the Third Invasion, cleared twelve plains and made four lakes. When he died the Fomhoire returned (this was the Fourth Invasion) and persecuted his followers. After an unsuccessful rebellion against the Fomhoire, Nemed's followers fled, some to Greece and some to the North of the World.

Those who had gone to Greece eventually returned in the Fifth Invasion. They were the Fir Bholg (or Firbolg), the Gailioin, and the Fir Dhomhnann. These peoples were probably historical as well as legendary. The Gailioin were also called the Laighin, who dwelt in the west in historical times and after whom Leinster was named; the Fir Dhomhnann were the people the Romans called the Dumnonii, who migrated from Britain to Ireland. These peoples established the Irish monarchy as a sacred kingship and divided the land into its five provinces: Meath in the center, Ulster to the north, Leinster to the east, Munster to the south, and Connacht to the west.

The Sixth Invasion was that of the Tuatha De Danann. An interesting incident of the final battle which drove out the Fomhoire for good was the defeat of the demon Balar, whose single eye was so large that it took four men to raise its lid. The glance of this eye could paralyze an army, but as soon as it was opened Lugh shot a slingstone at it and pushed it out through the back of Balar's head, so that it disabled Balar's army.

The Seventh Invasion, the last, brought to Ireland the Gaels who are still its chief inhabitants. They called themselves the Sons of Mil Espaine; hence the term "Milesians." "Mil Espaine" appears to be a Celtic pronunciation of the Latin *miles Hispaniae* ("soldier of Spain") and it was thought that the Romans' name for Ireland, Hibernia, was derived from their name for Spain, (H)iberia. Therefore the Gaels were said to have come from Spain.

After their defeat by the Gaels, the Tuatha De Danann refused to let the grain grow or the cows give milk unless they were granted part of the land. It was agreed that they could have half of Ireland, the lower half; and they retired underground, where, in the belief of many, they still live today.

Ultonian or Conorian Cycle

Cuchulain was in some ways the Irish Achilles: his life was fated to be as short as it was glorious. The Irish Helen, a woman whose beauty was fated to cause strife and suffering, was Deirdre, whose story appears in one of the *remhscela* ("previous stories") which precede the story of the Brown Bull of Quelny (or Cuailnge). Before Deirdre was born, a druid prophesied that she would be the most beautiful of women, but that her beauty would cause many sorrows. Some of King Conor's advisers wanted him to kill her at birth. He decided instead to have her raised by foster-parents, away from the sight of men, until she was old enough to marry him. (Theseus had had the same plan for Helen.) Having seen a raven feeding on the blood of a slain calf as it lay on the snow, Deirdre wished for a man who would have hair as black as the raven, cheeks as red as blood, and a body as white as snow. Her nurse, who was a witch, told her that this description fitted a man named Naoise. Deirdre put herself in Naoise's way and invited him to carry her off; but, knowing the prophecy about her and also being unwilling to betray his king, he refused until she accused him of cowardice. Then he agreed and with the help of his brothers carried her off to Scotland, where they remained in exile. Everywhere they went there was trouble, caused by Deirdre's fatal beauty. At last the friends of Naoise and his brothers prevailed upon Conor to allow their return, and the great hero Ferghus Mac Roich was sent to escort them and guarantee their safety. On their arrival in Ulster, Conor had the three brothers killed by his friend Eoghan Mac Durthacht and took Deirdre for himself. Ferghus was so insulted by this treachery that he left Conor and took his followers to the court of the Kings of Connaught.

After a year with Conor Deirdre was still weeping and mourning for her dead husband. When Conor asked her what she hated most in the world she replied, "You and Eoghan Mac Durthacht." To break her spirit Conor resolved to give her to Eoghan for a year but, as the three were traveling in a chariot, Deirdre committed suicide by leaping from the chariot and shattering her skull on a rock.

Ossianic Cycle

The adventures of Finn and his Fianna closely resemble, in their quests and adventures, those of Arthur and his knights. Unlike the heroes of the Ulster Cycle they had many dealings with the underground magical people who were the Tuatha De Danann. Like Arthur and his knights they were the protectors of their land from foreign invaders. Finn was also like Arthur in that he lost the love of his wife to his closest friend.

When Finn was growing old and had lost his first wife, Grainne was betrothed to him; but, like many other women, she was attracted to Finn's friend Diarmaid ua Duibhne, "Dermot of the Love Spot." At the wedding feast she administered a sleeping-potion to Finn and his guests, all but Dermot, on whom she cast an enchantment which forced him to elope with her. Aided by the love-god Angus, who was Dermot's foster-father, they always managed to escape Finn's pursuit. Finally Angus prevailed upon Finn to let Dermot and Grainne return.

When Dermot was invited to take part in the hunt of the magic boar of Beann Ghulban, his honor compelled him to accept even though he knew that he was fated to be killed by this animal, which had once been his foster-brother. He killed the boar but was badly wounded by it. Knowing he could be saved by a drink from the hands of Finn, who had the gift of healing, he asked Finn to go for water. Finn, hurried to a stream and started back with the water in his cupped hands but, remembering his old grievance, let it escape. A second time he returned to the river, but again his old hatred caused him to lose the water. The third time he brought the water but he was too late: Dermot was already dead.

Voyage of Maelduin

Travelers' tales of the wonders they have seen have always been fascinating. The real point of this otherwise rather pointless story is to provide a framework for descriptions of fabulous places. The same may be said of the voyages of Sinbad in *The Thousand Nights and a Night* of the Arabs or of *The Travels of Sir John Mandeville* which so fascinated xivth-Century Europe.

If we look at the *Odyssey* in the light of such tales, we can admire Homer for his skill in weaving these wonders into the fabric of his story so that they give a point to the whole, rather than remaining a mere list, as they do in the *Voyage of Maelduin*. The same is true to a lesser extent of Apollonius of Rhodes in his *Argonatica*. Both these authors must have used as part of their raw material just such stories as the Maelduin adventures.

King Arthur

Because we can trace the development of the Arthur legend much more clearly than we can any of the Greco-Roman myths, it may be worthwhile to look at it as an example of the creation of myth: how various elements can be brought together to form a fully developed story which is quite far from its historical origins.

The Roman army was withdrawn from Britain in A.D. 409, leaving the Romanized Celts and such Roman soldiers as had taken up residence there to resist the Saxon invaders. One of the battles in which they defeated the Saxons took place at Mount Badon in 516 and was mentioned in a book written ca. 540 by Gildas, who gave no name to the Romano-Celtic leader. But Nennius, in his history written in the early ixth Century, calls the general *Artorius* (a Latin name). He is mentioned again, this time as *Arturus*, as the Celtic general at Mount Badon in a book of the xth Century, which adds the information that he and Medraut (who later appears as Modred) died at the Battle of Camlann, in a civil war begun by Medraut in 537.

From the time of his death stories began to be told by the Celts about this great champion of their race; like Hercules, he seems to have attracted to himself many tales that were originally told of other heroes. Eventually he became a kind of Celtic Hercules or Theseus, traveling about and destroying various monsters such as the Demon Cat of Losanne, the monstrous boar Twrch Trwyth, and the Black Witch of Hell.

In the xth-Century *Spoils of Annwn* he is a Celtic Ulysses, raiding the land of the dead for the cauldron which magically fed brave men and returning with only six of his crew. He appears as a king holding court in *Culhwch and Olwen* (xith Century). He now has a wife Gwenhwyfar (Guinevere). His followers already include the heroes Cei (Kay), Bedwyr (Bedivere), Gereint (Gareth), Gwalchmai (Gawain), Llenlleawc (Lancelot), and Drwst (Tristan). Arthur's court (like the voyage of the Argonauts) became a place where all the important heroes were thought to have gathered, even when the chronology was thereby violated. We find that the early hero Manawyddan is there, along with Teyrnon, Pryderi's foster-father, and Gwynn (another name for Fionn or Fen). Finally he is provided, like Jason, with the Talented Companions of folk tale, such as Drem, who from Wales could see a fly in Scotland, and Clust, who could hear the movements of an ant fifty miles away.

Such tales as these were also current among the Celts of Brittany, and from there they spread through France and as far as Italy. The Cathedral of Modena has a sculpture (ca. 1100) showing Arthur, Kay, and Gawain rescuing Guinevere.

In 1125 William of Malmesbury reasserted Arthur's historicity, and deplored the fact that it was obscured by so many legendary tales. He was the first to mention the belief that Arthur was not really dead, but would return some day to rule his people again.

He appears as an historical figure in the *History of the Kings of Britain*, written ca. 1135 by Geoffrey of Monmouth. This "history," based, according to its author, on a book written in the Celtic language, has little in it which is historical, though it was accepted as true history for at least three centuries. According to Geoffrey, the first King of Britain was Brutus, a son of Silvius, the King of Alba Longa in Italy. It will be recalled that this Silvius was the son of Ascanius, the son of Aeneas the Trojan. Brutus had accidentally killed his father in a hunting accident and so went into exile with King Helenus in Chaonia. When Helenus died, his Trojan subjects were persecuted, so Brutus led them to Britain. Here he founded London, which he called New Troy, after having defeated the Giants, including Gog and Magog (actually figures from the Old Testament), sons of the Giant Albion, who had been slain by Hercules on his Tenth Labor. Britain took its old name, Albion, from him, but was now called Brutannia, and then Britannia, from Brutus.

Brutus' descendants by his Chaonian wife Imogen included King Bladud, the Celtic Daedalus, who devised many clever inventions but died from a fall while trying out some wings he had invented, and King Lear, whose story is well-known from Shakespeare's play. Lear's successors, Ferrex and Porrex, are the subjects of Sackville and Norton's play *Gorboduc*, the first tragedy written in English.

Geoffrey includes some figures who appear in other histories: he makes Brennus, the leader of the Gauls who sacked Rome in 387 B.C., and Cassivelaunus, who met Julius Caesar's second invasion of Britain in 54 B.C., descendants of Brutus.

When Britain became part of the Roman Empire, the dynasty founded by Brutus continued to reign as client-kings. That merry old soul King Cole was another of this line of kings. His daughter Helen (later canonized) married the Roman general Constantius and became the mother of the Emperor Constantine. The line of Brutus now ruled the Roman Empire. One of Constantius' descendants, Constans, was the father of Ambrosius, surnamed Uther, who was the father of Arthur.

Geoffrey's history makes Arthur rival Alexander the Great in his conquests: having driven out the Saxons, he conquered Scotland, Ireland, and Iceland. He sent out a call for allies, and all the greatest heroes of these lands, as well as many from all parts of the known world, came to join him and wear his uniform. With his followers he now conquered Norway, Denmark, and France.

Arthur's greatness attracted the attention of the Roman Emperor Lucius Hiberius (who existed only on Geoffrey's pages); he demanded tribute and when Arthur refused, led an army of 40,000 against him. The battle was fought in France; Lucius was defeated and killed. But when Arthur returned to Britain he found that his nephew Mordred had seized the kingship and married Arthur's wife Guinevere. Both Arthur and Mordred died in the battle of Camel.

In 1155 Geoffrey's history was translated into French as *Roman de Brut* , the "Story of Brutus." This was translated into English before 1200 by Layamon, who added the story that Arthur had seated his 1600 knights at a Round Table to avoid quarrels over precedence. He also wrote that Queen Morgan, a fairy, had taken Arthur to Avalon in a boat after the final battle with Mordred. Layamon called Brutus "Brute," the name by which he is usually known.

In the meantime, in the middle of the xiith Century, Chretien de Troyes in France had written a series of poems, not so much about Arthur as about his knights, basing them not on Geoffrey but on the tales and ballads of traveling bards. Chretien has none of the historical settings of Geoffrey: his events take place in a world that never was. It is in one of Chretien's stories that we first hear of the love affair of Lancelot and Guinevere.

Other writers over the next two centuries added details such as the test of the sword in the stone to the growing mass of literature about Arthur and his knights. Finally Malory's *Morte d'Arthur* (written in English despite its French title) in the xvth Century brought together Celtic, English, and French tales and traditions into one unified work, a masterful blending of history, myth, legend, romance, and folk tale. In it the great battle in France is not against a Roman emperor but against Lancelot and his knights, Lancelot having been forced into revolt by his love for Guinevere.

Malory's work was definitive but it was by no means the end of the development of the legend of Arthur. John Milton was fascinated by the stories and originally planned to write his great epic about Arthur instead of about the Fall of Man. Spenser makes use of Arthurian characters and incidents in *The Faerie Queen*. Tennyson retold many of the tales in his poetry, and the Arthurian legend was almost an obsession with the pre-Raphaelite artists and their literary counterparts. In our own century T. H. White retold the stories in the series of books published under the general title *The Once and Future King*; the musical *Camelot* is based on these. John Steinbeck wrote *The Acts of King Arthur and his Noble Knights*. Still more recently Mary Stewart has written a series of historical novels euhemerizing the stories: *The Crystal Cave, The Hollow Hills, The Last Enchantment,* and *Wicked Day.*

The Mabinogion

One of the most interesting of the stories occurs in the Fourth Branch, *Math Son of Mathonwy*; it is the story of Lleu Llaw Gyffes. King Math always had to have his feet resting in the lap of a virgin. When this court position was offered to his niece Arianrhod, she failed the test of virginity by giving birth to twins, whom her brother Gwydion had magically sired without her knowledge. One of these boys was named Dylan; he immediately plunged into the sea and became a sea-god. Because of her shame at having given birth to these unexpected children, Arianrhod pronounced a curse upon the other: he was to remain nameless unless she herself gave him a name and this she refused to do. But his father Gwydion disguised his son and himself as shoemakers, magically making from seaweed shoes that appeared to be of Cordovan leather. When Arianrhod ordered some of these shoes, they sent first too large and then too small a pair; she was forced to come down and be measured. While she was thus immobilized a wren alighted at some distance and the boy shot it with an arrow which passed through its leg between the sinew and the bone. She was impressed, and said, "The fair one (*lleu*) has hit it with a skillful (*gyffes*) hand (*llaw*)." Thus she was tricked into naming her son Lleu Llaw Gyffes.

Angered, Arianrhod now cursed her son with the curse that he would never bear arms until she armed him herself. Again Gwydion tricked her with his magic powers. He caused a great army of invaders to appear, and in this apparent emergency Arianrhod ordered all the men about her to be armed, including Lleu; the army immediately disappeared. She then cursed her son again, this time that he should not find a wife among the human race. With the help of Math, Gwydion made a beautiful woman from the flowers of the oak, the broom, and the meadowsweet; they called their creation Blodeuwedd ("Flower-Aspect"). Lleu was happy with his beautiful wife, but on one occasion when he was away she was unfaithful to him. She and her lover, Gronw Pebyr, decided to kill Lleu.

Killing Lleu was difficult, since (like Achilles and Siegfried) he was almost invulnerable. Gwydion's magic could not protect him absolutely, but he had established conditions for his wounding which were most unlikely to be satisfied. He could be harmed only by a spear which had taken a year to make, working on it only on Sundays during the brief moment of the Elevation of the Host at the Mass. He could not be killed on horseback nor on foot, inside or outside of a house. Like Delilah or Kriemhild, Blodeuwedd persuaded her husband, by expressing concern for his safety, to reveal the secret to her and even to demonstrate it by assuming the required position. He stood with one foot on a slain stag and the other in a cauldron which had been used as a bath and had hence been given a thatched roof. Gronw had in the meantime spent a year making the spear; he poisoned the head of it and wounded Lleu as he stood in the fatal position.

Lleu turned himself into an eagle and flew away, but the poison was eating into his flesh. When Gwydion eventually found the bird it was almost dead. He coaxed the bird from the oak tree where it was perching and, holding it in his lap, restored it to human form. Lleu was so wasted that it took a year to nurse him back to health. When he was well he sought out Gronw and aimed his spear at him. Gronw dodged behind a boulder but the spear passed through the rock and killed him.

In the meantime Gwydion had found Blodeuwedd. He said to her, "I will not kill you; I will do something worse: I will let you go in the form of a bird." He then turned her into an owl, the bird of darkness which the other birds hate.

The Little People

Some of the Daoine Sidh, "Deeny Shee," Little People, or "Gentry" of Ireland are undoubtedly the Tuatha De Danann, occupying their half of the island. Others, however, are thought to be the Firbolg; it may be that survivors of all the first six invasions belong to this underground race.

In other lands, although the habits and habitats of the fairies are strikingly similar, different origins are assigned to them. Their names in Italian, Spanish, and French (*Fata, Hada,* and *Fee*) are derived from the Latin *Fata,* the Fates. That these prankish spirits should be the grim Clotho, Lachesis, and Atropos seems unlikely, but they have one point in common, their association with the destinies of children. The Fates spinning and singing their prophetic song of the destiny of Achilles at the wedding of Peleus and Thetis (Catullus 64) are strikingly similar to the fairies who gather at the christening in the tale of *Sleeping Beauty,* one of whom, the malicious Carabosse, later disguises herself as a spinner. From the Fate who prophesies the child's future at his christening, it is not a great step to the Fairy Godmother.

The English name for a fairy, "Fay," is of the same derivation; but the name was brought to England by the Normans and applied to a race of spirits which was already in existence there. These were probably originally the spirits of the dead and their guardians, rather than diminished gods. The word "Fairy" originally referred to their realm, meaning "Land of the Fays," just as Judea was earlier called "Jewry."

In Scotland as well, the highland "People of Peace" and the lowland "Good Neighbors" were apparently originally the spirits of the recently dead, not allowed to leave this world until they had finished their business here.

Throughout the Celtic areas a new theory of the origin of the fairies came with the rise of Christianity: they are fallen Angels who have not fallen quite so far as the Devils. Some of the Angels who warred against God were not Lucifer's confederates, but only his dupes. As the defeated host fell in a long stream from Heaven to Hell, the most guilty fell first. At a certain point the Father, appealed to by the Son, arrested their fall, and each Fallen Angel now inhabits the realm in which he found himself at that moment: some are in the upper air, some on earth, and some underground; only the very wicked are confined to Hell.

In northern mythology the Light Elves and the Dark Elves, as well as the Trolls, existed already alongside the gods, inhabiting three of the Nine Worlds. But the Scandinavian countries have added to these beings the "Hidden People," the Huldre. These are descended from Adam and his first wife, Lilith; or else they are children of Eve whom she hid from God because she was ashamed of having so many children.

Modern scholars have many theories about the origin of the belief in fairies. Besides the spirits of the dead, deified ancestors, or diminished gods, they have been considered to be totemic spirits, animistic spirits, nuministic spirits, elementals, or hazy recollections of aboriginal races.

PRACTICAL APPLICATIONS

_____ Specific Literary References _____

1. In Ireland, a fairy shoemaker.

2. One of the priests of the Celtic gods.

3. Avilion or Avalon was the island where Arthur was taken by the fairies. It is often connected with the Fortunate Isles or the Islands of the Blest.

4. The greatest of King Arthur's knights.

5. The chalice of the Last Supper.

6. The largest and most elaborate arrangement of the Standing Stones which are found throughout the Celtic areas.

7. One of the euphemistic names for the Fairies.

8. Arthur's wife and queen.

9. The knights of King Arthur were seated for their meals at a great round table; hence they were called the Knights of the Round Table.

10. The two bulls of the Ultonian Cycle.

_____ Word Study _____

2. "Seat" (still its meaning in French).

3. The passage which explains the origin of fairies as diminished gods.

4. A group of stories linked together to provide a continuous narrative.

A story of heroic deeds, especially one which centers about one particular character and draws its details from other stories. Stories which every apprentice bard was required to know.

_____ Questions for Review _____

1. & 2. A branch of the great Indo-European-speaking family which moved westward across Europe from north of the Black Sea, ending up in what are now France, Spain, and the British Isles, and Ireland.

3. They were tall and red-haired, fond of war and of the ability to speak well, eager for news, easily influenced, optimistic, volatile, fond of change and display, quick and intelligent.

4. Through the testimony of Roman writers and through archaeological studies.

5. Making stones objects of veneration and believing in their magical powers.

6. A group of priests of the Celts.

7. The transmigration of souls.

8. The _Cycle of the Invasions of Ireland,_ the _Ultonian_ or _Conorian Cycle,_ the _Ossianic_ or _Fenian Cycle,_ the _Voyage of Maelduin,_ the _King Arthur Saga,_ and the _Mabinogion._

9. Dana, the Dagda, Angus, Midir, Lir, Manannan, the Morrigu, Bran, Gwydion, and Lugh.

10. The People of Dana.

11. As the Little People.

12. The Ultonian or Conorian Cycle.

13. The Red Branch.

14. He served some time as the watchdog (_Cu_) of Cullan (_Chulain_).

15. The Queen of Connaught.

16. The Brown Bull of Quelgny.

17. He fought the forces and the champions of Connaught single-handedly while the Ulstermen were prevented by a curse from fighting.

18. He was first overcome by magic.

19. The chief of a Fianna, a band collected to protect Ireland.

20. Ossian; Oscar.

21. He killed three kings in his first fight, and thereafter always fought with great bravery.

22. He had to be a poet, learn the *Twelve Books of Poetry*, defend himself against nine warriors while buried up to the waist, leap over a strip of wood level with his brow, run at full speed under one level with his knee, and pull a thorn from his foot while running.

23. The son of a great hero.

24. To avenge his father's death.

25. The Islands of Ants, of the Beast, of Demons, of the House of Invisible Spirits, of the Magical Apples, of Monsters, of Hot Earth, of the House of the Cat, of the Underworld, of Lamentation, of Laughter, of the Enchantress, and of the Fairy Fortress; he also saw a land under the sea.

26. In Britain.

27. Guinevere.

28. A table around which Arthur assembled his knights.

29. Lancelot; Galahad.

30. The Quest of the Holy Grail.

31. He died or left this world in battle with his nephew Modred.

32. Wales.

33. Pwyll, Pryderi, Bran, Manawyddan, Math, and Gwydion.

34. As the diminished gods of a conquered people.

35. A fairy shoemaker.

36. By fairy rings.

37. May Eve, Midsummer Eve, and November Eve.

_____ Reading List _____

Novels and Tales

Arthurian legend is applied to a contemporary setting in Charles Williams' *War in Heaven* and C. S. Lewis' *That Hideous Strength*.

The story of Lleu Llaw Gryffes provides the background for Alan Garner's moving novel *The Owl Service*; this book is of particular interest to adolescents. Two other books of Mr. Garner's, *The Weirdstone of*

Brisingamen and *The Moon of Gomrath,* make extensive use of Celtic (and to some extent Norse) mythology.

The *Prydain* cycle of books by Lloyd Alexander is set in the world of Welsh mythology.

Fairies who are the diminished gods of all nations (including the Greek gods) appear in *Island of Mist,* a fairy tale by the well-known ancient historian W. W. Tarn.

Conclusion: Other Applications of Mythology

PRACTICAL APPLICATIONS

_____ References to Mythology in Literature _____

1. The Pleiades.

2. The Chair of Cassiopeia, the mother of Andromeda, is one of the northern constellations.

3. The constellation Sagittarius is the Centaur Chiron.

4. Castor and Pollux.

5. The belt of Orion.

_____ Word Study _____

2. The practice of explaining myths as exaggerated accounts of historical events.

3. Human beings cannot help mythologizing their observations of the universe. Yes.

_____ Questions for Review _____

1. By saying that they actually dealt with the doings of human beings who had later been deified.

2. By claiming that the idea of personality had been attached to words of masculine or feminine grammatical gender.

3. Anthropology.

4. That different mythologies have much in common.

5. The belief that the life of animals and even of inanimate objects is of the same kind as human life. The belief that certain inanimate objects are inhabited by spirits. The belief in, and worship of, an animal as a tribal ancestor.

6. Creation myths, heaven-and-hell myths, myths of the flood, solar myths, lunar myths, hero stories, beast tales, soul myths, myths of journeys to and in the land of the dead. War gods, weather gods,

wind gods, thunder gods, gods of agriculture, gods of the chase, gods of death.

7. Milton, Shelley, Irving, Barrie, Dunsany.

8. To associate with the product some of the powerful archetypal ideas embodied in myths.

9. Many myths end with someone or something being carried to the sky to become a constellation.

_____ Reading List _____

To the list of modern myths may be added: the *Oz* books; George MacDonald's *The Princess and the Goblin, Curdie and the Princess, At the Back of the North Wind*, and numerous fairy tales; Tolkien's *The Hobbit* and the *Lord of the Rings* trilogy; C. S. Lewis' *Narnia* books and his trilogy, *Out of the Silent Planet, Perelandra*, and *That Hideous Strength*; and the novels of Charles Williams: *Descent into Hell, All Hallows' Eve, War in Heaven, Many Dimensions, The Place of the Lion*, and several others.

REVIEW MATERIAL

_____ References to Mythology in Literature _____

1. The Muses.

2. Mythical creatures, half man, half horse.

3. In Greek mythology the primeval mixture of all the elements.

4. The god or king of the winds.

5. Also called Diana, the goddess of the chase.

6. Supernatural bird-women who lured sailors onto the reefs by singing an irresistible song.

7. King of Ithaca, a character in the *Iliad* and the hero of the *Odyssey*, also called Ulysses.

8. Also called Jupiter, the god of the sky, the king and father of gods and men.

9. Clytie was the nymph who went mad for love of Apollo and was changed into a sunflower.

10. Apollo, god of the sun, of music, of prophecy, of sickness and health.

11. The goatish god of herdsmen and flocks; fresh-water nymphs; tree-nymphs.

12. The elderly satyr who was Dionysus' foster father.

13. The West Wind; the Roman goddess of flowers.

14. Helen of Troy, whose abduction by Paris caused the Trojan War.

15. The Ferryman who carries souls to the Dwelling of Hades.

16. Monstrous winged women with snaky hair and bronze claws; many-headed serpents; monsters part lion, part serpent, and part goat.

17. Gods of love; gods of marriage.

18. See #6; son of Peleus and Thetis, hero of the *Iliad*.

19. The part of the Lower World set apart for punishment.

20. The three-headed dog who guarded the entrance to the Lower World.

21. Son and mother, both gods of Love; also called Cupid and Venus.

22. Zeus, Pluto, and Poseidon divided the universe among them.

23. Goddesses of history, poetry, song, dance, drama, and astronomy.

24. Roman nature-gods, young men with some goat-like features; the Greek god of wine, milk, and sap.

25. Roman goddess of fruits; Roman god of wine.

26. Pursued by Apollo and Pan respectively, Daphne was changed into a laurel tree and Syrinx into a bed of reeds.

27. One of the rivers of the Lower World; foul bird-women who snatched away food; many-headed serpents.

28. The god of wine.

29. A daughter of the Sun, a great enchantress; see #6; fresh-water nymphs; the abode of the Blest in the Lower World; a monster who clung to the rocks and snatched six sailors from passing ships with her six dog-like heads; a monster who caused a whirlpool by swallowing and regurgitating the waters of the sea.

30. Goat-like Greek nature gods; their Roman equivalent, somewhat less animal-like.

31. A guardian spirit.

32. See #16.

33. Jupiter, the chief Olympian; the chief Titan.

34. God of dreams.

35. See #23 and #16.

36. Female spirits of water, trees, and mountains.

37. The great singer and poet who won permission to bring his wife back from the dead; belonging to Elysium, the abode of the blest; god and king of the Lower World; Orpheus' wife, who was forced to return to the dead when he looked back at her too soon.

38. See #4.

39. The metamorphosis of Daphne into a laurel tree when pursued by Apollo.

40. Minerva disguises herself to warn Arachne.

41. Neptune's trumpeter; the sea-god who could assume any shape.

42. Goddess of the chase; goddess of charm and love; female nature-spirit; the greatest of singers and poets.

43. Juno, the queen of the gods, was Junoesque in her height and in her dignified movements.

44. The two-faced Roman god of gateways and beginnings; the grave and wise old hero at the Trojan War.

45. The mountain reaching to the sky on which the Olympian gods lived.

46. The sun-god permitted his son Phaethon to drive his chariot; he lost control and the earth was scorched.

47. Apollo loved the boy Hyacinth; Narcissus loved himself.

48. The Roman goddess of war.

49. The Giants, sons of Gaea who made war on the Olympians.

50. Narcissus, who fell in love with his own reflection.

_____ Word Studies _____

1. Jove, Mercury, Vulcan, Ceres, Hercules, Vesta, Vulcan, Mars.

2. A beautiful young man; the ability to become wealthy effortlessly;

tranquil, happy times; anything which appeases whoever or whatever is blocking the way; a paradise; a very difficult riddle.

3. & 4. Answers will vary. Have students explain their choices.

5. *a.* Performing a task or solving a problem which is the result of long neglect, mismanagement, or misbehavior (from Hercules' Fifth Labor, which required him to remove the droppings of 3000 cattle accumulated over thirty years). *b.* Anyone's one vulnerable spot or weakness; from the spot not covered when Thetis dipped Achilles into the Styx to make him invulnerable. *c.* Asleep; Morpheus was the god of dreams. *d.* Faced with a dilemma; in passing through the straits of these two monsters a captain had to choose whether to lose at least six men or risk the entire ship. *e.* With unlimited wealth; Midas turned everything he touched into gold. *f.* She was a large, muscular or mannish woman; the Amazons were female warriors. *g.* A physician; Aesculapius was the god of medicine. *h.* Very beautiful; Helen of Troy was the most beautiful woman in the world. *i.* Very devious; Ulysses was known for his ability to outwit others and to extricate himself from difficult situations. *j.* Very strong; Hercules was the strongest man in the world.

6. Answers will vary.

_____ Comprehension Exercises _____

A. Questions for Review

1. The return of Persephone, the rebirth of Adonis [the marriage of Frey]; Clytie, Hyacinthus, Narcissus, Adonis; Phosphor, Hesper, Sirius, Pleiades (Phosphor and Hesper are in fact both the planet Venus); Pandora, Apollo, Artemis [Aesculapius and Medusa's blood]; Tithonus; Phaethon; Narcissus; Apollo and Daphne, Phaethon, Philemon and Baucis [Adonis].

2. Greek: Heaven and Earth emerged from primal chaos and produced the Titans. Norse: Midgard was created from the body of Ymir. Celtic: Unknown.

3. Jupiter: bull, shower of gold [Amphitryon, swan, eagle]. Cadmus and Harmonia: serpents. Callisto and Arcas: bears. Philemon: oak. Baucis: linden. Arachne: spider. Adonis: anemone. Atalanta and Hippomenes: lions. Statue Galatea: living Galatea. Rustics who mocked Latona: frogs. Hyacinthus: iris. Sisters of Phaethon: poplars. Orion [Cepheus, Cassiopeia, Perseus, Andromeda, sea-monster]:

constellation. Orion's dog Sirius: star. Pleiades: doves, then stars. Niobe: fountain. Nereus and Proteus: anything they pleased. Nymph Scylla: monster Scylla. Dionysus: lion [bull, panther]. Pirates: dolphins. Various possessions of Midas: gold. Io: heifer. Syrinx: reeds. Daphne: laurel tree. Clytie: sunflower. Nymph Echo: echo. Narcissus: narcissus. Tithonus: grasshopper. Ceyx and Halcyone: kingfishers. Orpheus' lyre: constellation. Phineus and followers, Polydectes and followers: stone. Dragons' teeth: armed warriors. Some of Ulysses' men: swine. Ymir: Midgard. Two trees: Ask and Embla. Angus' kisses: birds. [Nisus' daughter: sea bird. Perdix: partridge. Ino: Leucothea. Melicertes: Palaemon. Actaeon: stag. Lycaon: wolf. Adonis' mother: myrrh- or myrtle-tree. White bird: raven. Acis: river. Nymph Sirens: bird-women Sirens. Glaucus: merman. Minyades: bats. Marsyas: river. Clouds: false "Hera." Beautiful Medusa: monster Medusa. Medusa's blood: serpents and lizards. Ascalaphus: owl. Cycnus: swan. Medea's old he-goat: young kid. Seven birds and a snake at Aulis: stone. Companions of Diomedes: herons. Hecuba: dog. Polydorus: trees. Aeneas' ships: sea-nymphs. Vertumnus: old woman. Jotunns: eagles, wolves. Gullveig: three different shapes. Berry juice: Kvasir. Odin, Suttung: eagles. Loki: mare, fish. Hreidmar's son: otter. Andvari: fish. Fafnir: dragon. Sigurd: false "Gunnar." Dermot's foster-brother: boar of Bean Ghulban. Dylan: sea-god. Seaweed: Arianrhod's shoes. Flowers of oak, broom, and meadowsweet: Blodeuwedd. Blodeuwedd: owl. Lleu Llaw Gyffes: eagle]

4. Prometheus and fire, Deucalion and Pyrrha (Jupiter), Europa (Jupiter), Cadmus (Minerva), Baucis and Philemon (Jupiter and Mercury), Adonis (Venus), Psyche (Cupid), Atalanta and Hippomenes (Venus), Pygmalion and Galatea (Venus), Hyacinthus (Apollo), Marpessa (Apollo), Idas (Neptune), Coronis (Apollo), Admetus and Alcestis (Apollo), Endymion (Diana), Midas (Bacchus), Narcissus (Echo), Tithonus (Aurora), Ceyx and Halcyone (Jupiter, Juno, Aeolus), Orpheus (Pluto and Persephone), Danae (Jupiter), Perseus (Minerva, Mercury), Bellerophon (Minerva), Hercules (Minerva, Helios), Jason (Juno, Minerva), Paris (Venus), Ulysses (Minerva), Aeneas (Venus). Pandora (Jupiter), the Flood (Jupiter), Cadmus and Harmonia (Mars), Arachne (Minerva), Psyche (Venus), Atalanta and Hippomenes (Venus), the rustics of Lycia (Latona), Hyacinthus (Zephyrus), Idas (Apollo), Aesculapius (Jupiter), Endymion (Jupiter), Niobe (Latona, Apollo, Diana), Oeneus (Diana), pirates (Bacchus), Midas (Apollo), Hercules (Juno), Agamemnon (Diana), Orestes (Furies), Ulysses (Neptune), Aeneas (Juno).

5. The burning of the log which contained his life. This was Juno's

punishment for her abetting Jupiter in his amours. Quadrennial panhellenic athletic contests held during a universal truce. Phaethon and Asclepius. Hercules. The Nemean Lion, the Lernaean Hydra, the Arcadian Stag, the Erymanthian Boar, the Augean Stables, the Stymphalian Birds, the Cretan Bull, the Horses of Diomedes, the Girdle of Hippolyte, the Oxen of Geryon, the Apples of the Hesperides, Cerberus. By forgetting to change the black sails of his ship for white ones. By killing the sea-monster which was about to devour her. Apollo. Once by the bite of a poisonous snake and once when he was bringing her back from the Lower World and turned to look at her too soon.

6. Oceanids, Nereids, Naiads, Oreads, Dryads (Hamadryads). The Graces, the Muses, the Fates, the Furies, the Satyrs, the Camenae, the Fauns, the Norns, the Valkyries.

7. Juno, Minerva, Neptune. Venus, Mars. [Only Minerva, Venus, and Mars actually engaged in physical combat.] The goddess Minerva. He was murdered by his wife Clytemnestra and her lover Aegisthus. She was reclaimed by her husband and returned to Sparta after many wanderings. Ulysses' son by Penelope.

8. Greek mythology begins with primal chaos, Norse with at least two worlds already in existence; Greek gods are immortal and ageless, Norse gods are ever young but doomed to die; Norse mythology has proportionately fewer tales of the doings of heroes and more about the activities of gods; the Norse have more gods of war, storms, and untamed elements; Jotunns are more important in Norse mythology than Giants are in Greek. Janus, Saturn, Ops, the Camenae, Fortuna, Bellona, Terminus, Silvanus, Faunus, Lupercus, Luperca, Pomona, the. Lares, the Manes, Father Tiber, Romulus/Quirinus, and the deified emperors.

9. Homer, Hesiod, Pindar, Aeschylus, Sophocles, Euripides, Theocritus, Catullus, Virgil, Ovid, Horace, Seneca, Chaucer, Marlowe, Shakespeare, Jonson, Spenser, Racine, Corneille, Milton, Drayton, Dryden, Pope, Goethe, Wordsworth, Byron, Shelley, Keats, Robert Browning, Elizabeth Barrett Browning, Longfellow, William Russell Lowell, William Morris, Swinburne, Dante Gabriel Rossetti, Tennyson, Matthew Arnold, Austin Dobson, Thomas Moore, Charles Kingsley, Walter Savage Landor, William Vaughn Moody, Bayard Taylor, Stephen Phillips, Alfred Noyes, Hilda Doolittle, Robert Graves.

10. Orion, Niobe, Midas, [Marsyas,] Cassandra. Niobe. Cassiopeia, Ulysses, the Trojans, [Laomedon,] Laocoon, Palinurus. Cadmus.

Callisto, Latona, Bacchus, Io, Echo, Hercules, Paris, the Trojans, Aeneas. Psyche, Atalanta and Hippomenes, [Diomedes, the women of Lemnos].

11. Cadmus, Apollo and Python, the Hesperides, Jason, Siegfried, Beowulf. [In Graeco-Roman mythology a "dragon" is merely a very large serpent, sometimes with poisonous breath; in Norse mythology it is a large lizard which breathes fire; in Celtic mythology, it is a large lizard with wings.]

12. Perseus, Theseus, Hercules, Jason, Ulysses, Aeneas, Maelduin, the Knights of the Round Table.

13. Orpheus, [Theseus,] Hercules, Aeneas.

14. Pandora, Psyche, Atalanta, Alcestis, Althaea, Halcyone, Medea, Helen, Penelope, Dido, Brunhild, Kriemhild, Guinevere[, Blodeuwedd].

15. Atalanta, Hercules, wedding of Peleus and Thetis.

16. He had a hundred eyes, some of which were always awake. Nereus and Proteus. The Augean Stables; [but the Lernaean Hydra and the Stymphalian Birds were both euhemerized in antiquity to signify the draining of swamps].

17. Answers will vary. Have students explain their choices.

18. Mars, Mercury, Jove, Venus. Martedi, Mercoledi, Giovedi, Venerdi (Italian); Mardi (as in Mardi Gras), Mercredi, Jeudi, Vendredi (French).

19. Suggested answers: Telephassa ("Far-Shining"), television; Eucinesia ("Easily Moving"), cinema; Teleboe ("Far-Shouting"), radio; Gelotographia ("Laugh-Drawing/Writing"), comic strips; Cordacismia ("Unseemly Motions"), rock music.

20. The Olympic Games

B. True/False

1. F	2. T
3. F	4. F
5. T	6. T
7. F	8. T
9. F	10. F

11. T	**12.** T
13. T	**14.** F
15. T	**16.** F
17. F	**18.** F
19. T	**20.** T

C. *Multiple Choice*

1. Bacchus
2. Mercury
3. goat
4. pomegranate
5. laurel
6. Lethe
7. sea monster
8. Muses
9. Gibraltar
10. north
11. because of the wiles of Medea
12. Venus
13. Agamemnon
14. Calypso
15. Evander

Costumes of the Greeks

The various sketches, plays, tableaux, and ballets suggested in the text can be much more effective with authentic costuming. In the case of classical myths and legends this is easy, since Greek clothing consisted of rectangular pieces of cloth draped, pinned, and girded in various ways. Hence appropriate costumes can be improvised from donated or borrowed bedspreads, sheets, tablecloths, and curtains. It may also be possible to buy cloth from your teaching aids budget and make costumes; this involves only cutting to size and turning the cut edges to prevent fraying. Since Greek garments fit all sizes, no retailoring is ever necessary and a useful collection of costumes can be accumulated over the years. Roman gods and heroes are always depicted in Greek dress (the toga was not introduced until the vith Century B.C.), so the costumes will do for all the classical myths. Plain colors appropriate to the person should be chosen, but there can be geometric or stylized floral borders.

There are five basic costumes, though they may be varied considerably in the draping, pinning, and girding: the peplum, the chiton, the exomis, the himation, and the chlamys.

The peplum was originally a Dorian garment. In its simplest form it is two rectangles of cloth, placed in front and in back of the body and pinned together on the shoulders, then girt around the waist. It is open at the sides, but may be wide and overlapped before the girdle is tied. The length can be adjusted by pulling it up through the girdle and allowing it to hang over. It was worn by both men and women, but in ancient art it is usually a feminine garment. There are two main variations. The peplum may be cut very wide and gathered on the shoulders before being pinned (see figures, pp. 133 and 148 in the text). It may also be cut very long and a portion of each piece folded over at the top, so that a kind of wide bib hangs down in front and in back (see p. 1). The back one can be pulled up to make a head-covering or veil (see figure, p. 182 [Medea]). Sometimes these folded-over pieces are quite long, down to the waist or hips. The peplum may be girt either around the waist or under the bosom, or both (see the third figure from the right in the color plate *Aurora*).

The Ionian equivalent to the peplum was the chiton. This is a single piece of cloth. The middle of one side is placed under the left arm, then the two top corners are pinned together under the right arm. The front and back are then pinned together on the shoulders and a girdle is put around the waist. Length and width have the same variations as with the peplum: the material may be gathered on the shoulders before being pinned, and the chiton may be pulled through the girdle to adjust the length. Hunters, shepherds, etc. use this method to shorten the hemline to just above the knee (see figures, pp. 130 [Charon], 135, and 222 [central boy]). As with the peplum, two girdles may be used, by women to make a kind of brassiere, and even by men to shorten the garment without too much blousing. The chiton differs from the peplum in appearance in two ways: its "armholes" are in the top of the garment instead of at the sides, making diagonal folds on the breast, and it is open only on the right side, rather than on both sides.

Smiths and others who must keep the right arm free wear the exomis. This is simply a smallish chiton from which the pin under the right arm and the pin on the right shoulder have been removed, allowing the top corners to hang free, front and back (see figures, pp. 59 and 191 [where Ulysses uses two girdles to shorten the exomis]). The double exomis is arrived at by taking out the remaining pin and allowing the garment to hang from its girdle bath-towel fashion.

The himation is a single rectangle, usually about two yards by four in size, though the feminine version may be narrower (and is often made of thinner material). The middle of one long side is placed under the right arm and the two ends are thrown over the left shoulder, with either the front end or the rear end on top. These ends may be kept on top of the left shoulder, allowed to cover the left shoulder and the left arm to the wrist (see figure, p. 128 [Pluto]), or allowed to slide from the left shoulder onto the left forearm. The movement of the left arm is hampered — for example, if it is lowered the himation may fall off — so in moments of exertion the ends may be wound around the left forearm (see the color plate of Jupiter and Ganymede). In repose the himation may be removed from the left shoulder (see figures, pp. 24 [Jupiter], 103, and 133 [Pluto]). Occasionally, for warmth, the right arm may also be brought inside the himation (see figure, p. 174 [Argonaut]). A fold of the himation (the part which goes from under the right arm around the back) may also be brought over the head (see figures, pp. 222 [Aeneas] and 232 [Tiber]).

The chlamys, worn by warriors and travelers, is a smaller rectangle, perhaps four or five feet by five or six. The middle of a long side is placed on the left shoulder and the front and back are pinned together on the right shoulder, allowing a fairly large neck opening (see figure, p. 191 [Ulysses' men]). The middle of the other long side is brought up and placed on the left forearm, allowing the bottom corners to hang down to the calves, and the upper corners to hang loose over the breast and back.

These garments may be worn in various combinations. For the himation worn over the peplum, see the colored plate of the Sibyl and the figures on pp. 70 and 160 (Athena). For the himation worn over the chiton, see Aurora in the colored plate and the figures on pp. 24 (Juno), 43, 44, 52, 91, 100 (Maenads), 114, 128 (Hercules), 130 (lady), 142, 174, and 181 (lady). The himation may also be rolled or twisted and used as a girdle for the chiton (this is to get it out of the way for strenuous activities (see the color plate of Diana and the figure on p. 248 [flute-player]). The chlamys worn over the chiton may be seen in the figures on pp. 181 (Jason), 182 (Jason), and 232 (shepherds).

Picture books of classical art are good sources to determine which costume is appropriate for which character, as are art museum catalogues and postcards. Not all the characters will be found, but common sense will help: Ajax would be dressed like Diomedes, Auge like Iole, etc.

Here are some general suggestions: soldiers, girt-up chiton and chlamys; hunters, girt-up chiton with or without the chlamys; travelers, chlamys, with or without the girt-up chiton; workers, single or double exomis; matrons, full gathered peplum or chiton and himation; maidens, peplum without overfold or chiton, narrow thin himation; older men, priests, and seers, chiton and himation; younger men, himation or chlamys; children, narrow chiton or peplum without overfold. Some suggested colors: soldiers, kings, and reigning queens, white and dark red; matrons and older men, grey, black, dark blue, white; brides, saffron; maidens, white and blue or rose; young men, orange, green, blue, violet; children, white or pastel colors; villains and crafty people, bright red; avaricious, greedy, and jealous people, yellow. These are only suggestions; more important is the appearance of the *ensemble*.

Gods can have their appropriate colors: sky gods, white, light blue, light yellow; earth gods, green and brown; water gods, green and blue; gods of the underworld, black; gods of love, yellow and green; gods of marriage, saffron. The costumes of the gods are like those of their human counterparts.

top row: left to right: chiton, exomis, chiton and chlamys **bottom row: left to right:** peplum with overfold, pleated peplum, peplum and himation

Index of Proper Names

Note: A pronunciation key is provided for those names not included in the student text.

A

Myrmidons (mur'-mi-donz) 100, 101
Mysia[n] (mī'-ze-yuh[n]) 78, 86, 91, 92, 96
Mysteries, Villa of 46

N

Nagelfar (nahg'-el-far) 139
Nanna (nahn'-nah) 136
Naoise (na-ō'-sē) 153
Narcissus 54, 55
Nauplius (naw'-plē-us) 94, 95, 96, 103
Nausicaa 110
Naxos 69, 71, 111
Neleus (nē'-lē-us) 78, 79, 85
Nemea[n] 37, 39, 57, 74
Nemed 152
Nemesis 15, 18, 54
Nemi (nā'-mē) 68
Nennius (nen'-nē-us) 155
Neoptolemus 95, 98, 99, 103, 104, 112
Nephele 85
Neptune 9, 11, 12, 27, 31, 38, 48–50, 53, 70, 74–79, 83, 103, 119, 120
Nereids 46, 49, 95
Nereus 46, 50, 77
Nero (nē'-rō) 130
Nessus 79, 81, 83
Nestor 41, 79, 92, 100, 103
Nibelungenlied 143, 146
Nibelungs 143, 147
Nicippe (nī-sip'-pē) 72
Nidhogg (nēd'-hog) 134, 135, 139
Niflheim 134, 135
Nimrod (nim'-rod) 42
Ninus (nī'-nus) 33
Niobe 41, 42, 59
Nisus 21
Njord (nyoor) 135, 136, 137
Noatun (nō'-ah-toon) 135
Norns 135, 139, 140
Norse[men] (nors['-men]) 4, 124, 133, 134, 136, 140, 141, 143, 146, 163
Notus 46
Nubia (nyoo'-bē-uh) 44
Numitor (num'-i-tor) 115
Nymphs 8, 13, 15, 17, 19

O

Oceanid[s] 46, 49, 65
Oceanus 7, 14, 38, 42, 46, 47, 49, 50, 53, 57
Od (ōd) 139
Odin 135, 136–146
Odysseus (Ulysses) 99, 107, 130
Odyssey 105, 106, 108, 109, 127, 130, 131, 154
Oeagrus (ē-ag'-rus) 61
Oechalia (ē-kal'-ē-yah) 78, 79
Oedipus 23–25, 27, 52, 68, 72, 73, 93

Oenomaus (ē-nom'-a-us) 53
Oenone (ē-nō'-nē) 94, 98
Oenopion (ē-nop'-ē-on) 40
Ogmios (og'-mē-os) 149, 150
Ogygia 104
Oileus (o-wī'-lē-us) 98, 103
Oisin (ō'-sin) 151
Olympiad 37, 40, 127
Olympian[s] 4, 7, 17, 18, 23, 57, 58, 71, 78, 79, 80
Olympic 37, 39, 40, 74, 80
Olympus 7, 10, 13, 14, 39, 75, 78
Omphale 78
Ops 119, 120, 121
Orchomenus (or-kom'-en-us) 52, 85, 87
Orcus (or'-kus) 63
Orestes 104
Orion 40, 42
Orpheum (or'-fē-um) 18
Orpheus 18, 41, 47, 61, 62, 64, 86, 88, 90, 92, 116, 129
Orphic 45, 51, 61, 62
Orthus (or-thus) 57, 74, 75
Osiris (ō-sī'-ris) 28
Ossian (Oisin) 151
Ossianic 151, 153, 161
Ossipaga (os-si-pā'-gah) 122
Ovid 30, 47, 54, 55, 121, 129, 131

P

Pactolus 85
Palaemon (pah-lē'-mon) 24, 120
Palamedes 94, 101, 103
Palatine (pal'-uh-tīn) 114, 118, 119, 120
Palinurus 116
Palladium (building) 18; (statue) 95, 98, 103
Pallas (Athena) 69, 125; (son of Evander) 114
Pallene (pal-lē'-nē) 76, 79
Pan (pan) 46, 48, 52, 56, 121, 125
Panacea (pan-uh-sē'-uh) 35
Panathenaic (pan-ath-uh-nā'-ik) 21
Pandora 9, 11
Panisci (pan-is'-kī) 121
Pantheon (pan'-thē-on) 128
Paon (pā'-on) 46
Paphus 29
Paris 93, 94, 97, 98, 100, 101, 109
Parnassian[s] 18
Parnassus 14, 18
Parthenope (par-then'-uh-pē) 47
Partholan 152
Pasiphae (pa-sif'-uh-ē) 8, 21, 23, 71, 75
Pegasus 65, 69, 71, 75
Peirene (pī-rē'-nē) 60
Peleus 15, 29, 41, 60, 78, 85, 92, 95, 100, 101, 104, 159
Pelias 29, 41, 84, 85, 89

Romulus 13, 114, 115, 116, 117, 120, 123
Romulus Silvius (sil'-vē-us) 115
Rosmerta (ros-mer'-tah) 150
Round Table 157, 160

S

Saliva 137
Salmydessus (sal-mē-des'-sus) 86
Salus (sal'-us) 35
Sammuramat (sam-moor'-uh-mat) 33
Sarpedon 22
Saturn 8, 11, 12, 118, 119, 120, 123, 124, 125
Saturnalia 8, 120, 124
Sciron (skī'-ron) 66, 71
Scorpion 42
Scylla 46, 47, 50, 88, 105, 112
Scyros (skī'-ros) 68, 95, 98, 104
Sebhka Farun (sev'-kah fah-roon') 87
Segesta (sē-jes'-tah) 113
Selene (suh-lē'-nē) 7, 40, 46, 58
Semele 23, 51
Seneca 30, 130
Septimius Severus (sep-tim'-ē-us se-veer'-us) 44
Seriphos (seh-rī'-fus) 65, 70
Sessrymnir (ses'-rim-neer) 135
Sestos 32
Sibyl[s] 22, 36, 112, 113, 114, 115
Sibylline 36, 45, 114
Sicharbaal (sik-har-bā'-al) (Sychaeus) 113
Siegfried 143, 147, 158
Sif (seef) 135, 136, 138
Sigi (sē'-gē) 143
Sigmund (sig'-mund) 143, 144
Signy (sig'-nē) 143, 146
Sigunn (sē'-goon) 138
Sigurd 143, 144, 145
Silenus 45, 48, 56, 121
Silvanus 121, 123, 124, 150
Silver Age 9, 15
Silvius (sil'-vē-us) 115, 156
Sinfiotli (sin'-fyot-lē) 143
Sinis (sin'-is) 37, 66, 71
Sinon 98, 102
Siren[s] 15, 46, 47, 49, 88, 107
Sirius 40
Sisyphus 40, 60, 62, 68, 94
Skade (skah'-deh) 135
Skidbladnir (shē'-blahd-neer) 135
Skuld (skool) 141
Sleipnir (slep'-neer) 142, 145
Soekkvabekk (sehk'-vah-bek) 135
Sol (sōl) 7
Somnus 62, 63
Spartoi (spar'-toy) 23
Sphinx 24, 25, 57
Statanus (sta-tā'-nus) 123

Stentor 100
Sthenelus (sthen'-uh-lus) 72
Stheno (sthen'-ō) 65
Strophades (strof'-uh-dēz) 86, 112
Stymphalian 82, 87
Stymphalides (stim-fā'-luh-dēz) 74
Styx 23, 51, 57, 63, 95
Sucellus (soo-kel'-lus) 150
Sulis (soo'-lis) 150
Surt (soort) 134, 140
Suttung (soot'-tung) 137
Svadilfari 145
Sychaeus (sik-ē'-us) 113
Symplegades 86, 92
Syrtes (sur'-tēz) 87, 88, 110, 116

T

Taenarum (tē'-na-rum) 57, 88
Talassio (ta-las'-sē-ō) 122
Talos (tal'-os) 21, 88
Tammuz (tahm'-mooz) 28, 31, 34
Tantalus 58, 59, 62, 116
Taranis 149, 150, 151
Tarquin (tar'-kwin) 36, 113, 121
Tartarus 58–60, 63
Tauri 108
Tegea (tej'-ē-uh) 79, 96
Telamon 41, 78, 85, 92, 98, 99
Teleboe (tel-uh-bō'-ē) 171
Telegonus (tel-eg'-o-nus) 106, 109
Telemachus 101, 106, 107, 108
Telephassa (tel-uh-fas'-suh) 171
Telephus (tel'-uh-fus) 79, 96
Telesphorus (tel-es'-fuh-rus) 35
Terminus 121
Terpsichore 15, 19
Tethys 7, 14, 38, 42, 47, 50, 53, 57
Teucer (tyoo'-sur) 112
Teutates 150
Teuthras (tyoo'-thras) 96
Teutonic (tyoo-ton'-ik) 2
Teyrnon (teh'-eer-non) 155
Thais (thā'-is) 99
Thalia (Grace) 15; (Muse) 15, 19
Thanatos 62, 63
Thea 7, 34, 40, 46
Theban 41, 66, 72
Thebe (thē'-bē) 96, 99
Thebes 21, 23, 27, 41, 59
Thelxiepeia (thelx-ē-uh-pē'-yah) 47
Themis (Carmenta) 114; (daughter of Ilus) 111; (Law-and-Order) 7, 9, 15, 17
Thera (thēr'-ah) 88
Theseus 21, 37, 41, 42, 59, 66, 67, 69, 71, 75, 77, 84, 85, 89, 92, 93, 95, 111, 143, 153, 155
Thessalian[s] (thes-sā'-lē-un[z]) 34
Thessaly 76, 84, 90